Fear NO Evil

Fear **NO** EVIL

The Story of Denny Nissley and Christ In Action

DENNY NISSLEY
with
Jodie Randisi

HAROLD
SHAW
PUBLISHERS

Wheaton, Illinois

ISBN 0-87788-260-6

Cover design by Tobias Design, Grand Rapids, MI.
Cover background photo by Mike Cosentino, Portraits of Ministry
Cover portrait photo by Sandy Nissley
Interior design and typesetting by Carol Barnstable

Library of Congress Cataloging-in-Publication Data

Nissley, Denny, 1955-
    Fear no evil : the story of Denny Nissley and Christ In Action /
    by Denny Nissley and Jodie Randisi.
      p.   cm.
    ISBN 0877882606 (pbk.)
    1. Nissley, Denny, 1955- . 2. Christian biography—United States.
    3. Narcotic addicts—United States Biography. 4. Alcoholics—United States
    Biography. I. Randisi, Jodie, 1957- . II. Title.
    BR1725.N53A3   1999
    277.3' 0825' 092—dc21   99-26637
                                                          CIP

03 02 01 00 99
10 9 8 7 6 5 4 3 2 1

Table of Contents

Acknowledgments

Rural southern Lancaster County, Pennsylvania, home of the Amish and the Pennsylvania Dutch, does not usually lead to a life of alcohol and drug addiction. However, that's the life I chose in spite of being raised in a churchgoing family with parents who loved me and did everything a parent could or should for me. Leaving the mainline denominational church and turning to the world, I was on a path of self-destruction. At age twenty-two I found myself addicted to alcohol and drugs and far from the teachings of my childhood. Then, on April 3, 1977, as the answer to the prayers of my father and mother, I was taken to church, a service held in a barn for a couple of hundred people who used to be just like me. I was taken there by a guy named Charlie. Little did I know that Charlie did the greatest single deed in my life by taking me to that barn that Sunday morning. That was the morning I surrendered my life to Jesus for the forgiveness of my sins and the restoration of everything in my life.

Since that Sunday in the barn in rural Pennsylvania, God has had a lot of "Charlies" in my life. Mark King, the pastor of the church in that barn shaped my early Christian life by persuading me to take God at His word and believe everything in the Bible as if it were intended for me personally. Then came Hank, a guy from the church in the barn who invited himself to move into my home and live with me so he could disciple me, since I was too young in the Lord to know how to live the Christian life. I don't know where I'd be today had Hank not obeyed God and laid down his life to train me. More "Charlies" were along the way in Christ for the Nations Bible School in Dallas, Texas. Had it not been for a fifteen-minute talk with a student leader, Mike Massa, I probably would not have gone into the ministry.

All along the way in my walk with God, there have been faithful people to see me through to the next level.

My dear friend David Beaulieu who encouraged me and gave me great advice as I was pioneering my ministry.

Pastor Jim Brankel, who took me under his arm and helped me get credentialed with the Assemblies of God. This man taught me how to deal with my first arrest for preaching the gospel.

God brought me alongside of Jonathan Gainsbrugh, one of the greatest street preachers of my generation. Jonathan taught me how to really work in conjunction with the local church and how to equip others to carry the wonderful message of the gospel.

How thankful I am for Pastor Gary Grogan, a man of God who helped me understand the art of interpersonal relationships and who set a godly example of servanthood.

It would take too much room to fully explain how I met Pastor Wendell Choy, from Hawaii, but as a result of my relationship with Wendell my family and I were able to live in Hawaii and establish a beachhead of ministry and outreach on three of the four major islands in that state. I am most thankful for the obedience of Pastor Choy and for that opportunity. Our fifth daughter, Leah, was born in Honolulu.

Living now in Virginia, I am thankful to have the best pastor I could ask for. Charles Nestor is a tremendous teacher and has offered guidance to me and my family.

Also in the Capitol area is my friend Rob Schenck, president of the National Clergy Council. Rob has opened many doors for me to minister on Capitol Hill. He has made it possible for me to minister to senators and representatives alike.

God has brought forward many people over the years who have stepped up to support this ministry. Most remarkable are the people like the Reverend P. A. Scroggins and Ray and Pearl Blevins, retirees who from their Social Security checks each month make sure they help this ministry. I have had folks write ten thousand dollar checks, but it's the older saints that bring a tear to my eye when I see the checks written in careful, shaking hands.

Then there are the Randisis. Joe and Jodie have been great friends for fifteen years. I have had hundreds of people over the years say, "Denny, you should write a book." My answer was always "I'm too busy trying to live one." Jodie decided to get the stories on tape and get this book out where others could be blessed—not blessed by Denny Nissley but blessed by the awesome power of God, by seeing how great and mighty God really is right now, not just in the days of the Bible. He is the same yesterday, today, and forever. This book is not a result of one man but rather a combination of all the people I mentioned and hundreds I haven't mentioned. It is truly a book on the body of Christ. I happen to be the guy in the pit while all of these other people are holding the rope.

The single greatest person God has brought into my life is my wife, Sandy. The apostle Paul says that if we are married, our interests are divided. He is right, but I would not be the man I am today had God not brought Sandy into my life. My wife is my best friend and my greatest critic. When all others are gone, she is still there telling me not to grow weary and to preach one more time. She is the mother of our ten children and the backbone of our family. She is the one who launches me out into even greater things for God. When I come to her with some insane idea like preaching at the KKK rally or the Million Man March, she is the first one to say "go preach real good, honey." As Scripture says, "A good wife who can find? Her worth is far above jewels." I found one!

My greatest desire is that by reading this book you will be inspired to allow God to totally control your life and use you in ways you never thought possible. If for some reason you don't know Jesus as your personal Lord and Savior, I pray that as you read these stories you will discover the God that I discovered and will desire to live for Him because He died for you.

Thank you for reading this book. Now it is your turn to help in the harvest field as together we become Christ . . . in action.

Denny Nissley

Introduction

Before his conversion in April of 1977, Denny Nissley was an incorrigible, shameless, callous criminal. His amazing transformation from a drug- and alcohol-addicted holy terror into an accomplished and wholly devoted man of God is a miraculous story worth telling, and one very much worth reading.

Today Denny is an ordained Assemblies of God minister and a master evangelist. His ministry, Christ In Action, is engaged in today's culture accomplishing what few have done in the arena of street ministry and evangelism. As a minister of the gospel, Denny will do whatever it takes to win the lost, including feeding entire neighborhoods. (It's hard for unbelievers to speak unfavorably about Christians with their mouths full of free food.) He often carries a ten-foot wooden cross and preaches over a portable public address system while soul winners from Christ In Action pass out colorful, contemporary gospel tracts in hopes of starting conversations about Christ. Christ In Action has sponsored and organized scores of major outreaches in forty-nine of the fifty United States, in Canada, and in England.

Denny disagrees with those who say faith is a

private matter. For him, attracting people to Christ is a very public matter, perhaps because he's notably qualified to reach unlikely candidates for conversion, people who would probably never darken the doorway of a church. Denny has ministered to prostitutes, pimps, and professional hitmen, countless drug addicts, gang members, and alcoholics, as well as numerous business people, diplomats, representatives, and senators. He has been shot at, put in jail, threatened with knives, and beaten unconscious for preaching the gospel. His involvement in launching evangelistic ministries along with his dedicated, skilled effort to pioneer churches, brought him national recognition in 1991 when he was awarded an honorary Doctorate of Evangelism from Columbia Evangelical Seminary in Longview, Washington.

Who would marry a radical sold-out street preacher such as Denny Nissley? Denny hadn't given it much thought until he met a student from Christ for the Nations Bible School named Sandy James. In 1981, Denny was a twenty-six-year-old, fiery street preacher and the self-appointed president of the Bachelor Till the Rapture Club dedicated to doing as much damage as he could in the devil's own territory on the streets of America. Denny was sure God hadn't made a woman who could tie him down. The amazing part is not that he gave up bachelorhood but that he proposed to Sandy on their second date and they were married after being in each other's presence only six times! Denny met Sandy in New Orleans on a Mardi Gras outreach; he realized who she was in Lancaster, Pennsylvania; they had their first date in Washington, D.C.; he proposed in Illinois; she got her engagement ring in Tulsa, Oklahoma; they got married in Cleveland, Ohio; and had wedding receptions in Ohio, Pennsylvania, Oklahoma, and Colorado. In Frog Hollow, Virginia, they found out they were expecting their first child, and Rachel Nissley was born in Greeley, Colorado. All of that took place within a span of eighteen months. Eighteen years later, they have ten children—nine daughters and one son. Amazingly, this prolific pace is also representative of the Nissleys' drive and passion for bringing people to the Lord.

If some marriages are made in heaven, then this is one of them. And if God ordains men and women to be together in life and ministry, then there's no doubt He handpicked this couple. Unquestionably, their union was destined for God's glory. Since the very beginning of their life together, Denny and Sandy Nissley have continually experienced God's goodness and supernatural blessings. And every year on September 12 the Nissleys celebrate the day the President of the Bachelor Till the Rapture Club listened to the Holy Ghost, gave up the post, and tied the knot.

With his family by his side, Denny travels across America in a motorcoach not only to preach the gospel but also to inspire believers to become Christ in action. As a "missionary to America and beyond," he encourages Christians to take the love of Jesus to where it's most desperately needed and hardest to find. He schedules outreaches to coincide with established major events such as Mardi Gras, the Indy 500, the Boston Marathon, Spring Break at Daytona Beach, state fairs, and even KKK rallies. He also creates events known as Family Fests where he works in conjunction with local churches interested in reaching their communities for Christ. Furthermore, whenever there's a natural disaster, such as a tornado or flood, teams of volunteers from Christ In Action provide relief to victims and minister to them spiritually. For me, Denny's deep devotion to sharing Christ with those least likely to pursue religious contact is invigorating. No matter what type of ministry is being done, Denny's primary concern is to bear fruit that remains. That's why he works with a vast network of churches across America connecting new believers with local pastors. Denny assures each convert the opportunity to begin his or her new life in Christ on solid ground.

The stories in this book are true. As a friend and long-time supporter of the Nissleys, I've been listening to and collecting these stories for over fif-

teen years. I knew that someday they would be a part of demonstrating God's affinity for using ordinary people to accomplish extraordinary things. Each anecdote dramatically portrays and highlights Denny's "Holy Ghost hutzpah." His passion is contagious, his methods unconventional and engaging. No matter what he does, he captures the attention of those around him in order to direct them towards a personal relationship with the Lord Jesus Christ. Denny's stories verify that the power of God is available to those who dare to put their trust in God alone. Believers in Christ can rest assured that greater is He who is in us than he who is in the world.

Jodie Randisi*

*Introductions to chapters appear in italic type and are written from the perspective of Jodie Randisi.

CHAPTER ONE

A Funnel for Beer, or for Blessings?

Denny Nissley is a master storyteller with an abundance of marvelous stories to relate, but there's one particular story that he repeats more than all the others, and that is his testimony of how he became a Christian. Although raised in a loving Christian home in Pennsylvania, he was determined not to be like those "Jesus freaks," a phrase that in Denny's terms referred to anyone who had the gall to talk about Jesus as if He was real!

The stark contrast of Denny's wild rebellious days to his outcome as the founder and director of Christ In Action Ministries clearly demonstrates God's goodness, His grace, and unconditional love. Denny has given his dramatic testimony on Christian radio and television talk shows and has been featured on both The 700 Club *and the Canadian television program,* 100 Huntley Street. *When he speaks to church congregations and Christian organizations across America, audiences are enthralled with his fascinating stories. The best place to begin, however, is at the beginning.*

The first time I got drunk I was thirteen years old. My buddies and I camped out at the edge of the Susquehanna River so that when five o'clock in the morning came we could have our hooks in the water for the first moments of trout season. Someone brought six bottles of Boone's Farm apple wine and as a result, I never saw a fish or laid hands on a fishing rod.

The wine tasted so sweet. Even after consuming an entire bottle, it didn't seem to bother me—until I stood up. Then it hit me like a ton of bricks. The world spun out of control and trees began to multiply. As I tried to decide which tree to grab for support, I quickly lost control. While throwing up, I thought, *I'm miserable! Why would anyone like getting drunk? I'll never do this again.*

But deep down inside I knew I would do it again, even though the next morning my head throbbed, my stomach ached, and I felt as if an army of ants with muddy boots had run through my mouth. Unfortunately my friends at school made the mistake of asking me, "Hey, Denny, what'd you do this weekend?"

> Deep down inside I knew I would do it again.

"Oh, a bunch of us partied down by the river and I got stinkin' drunk. I was smashed out of my mind!" I bragged.

"Really? Wow, that's cool!" They encouraged me.

Instantly, I had a reputation to live up to and felt obligated to go when invited to weekend beer parties. By the time I was sixteen I was drinking and doing drugs constantly. Getting stoned on pot at school was my normal routine, but because I was a member of the wrestling team, I kept myself from going wild during the week. Besides, alcohol, not drugs, was the object of my heart's desire.

Over the years I progressed from being a drug and alcohol user to a hard-core drug and alcohol abuser, an addict. I successfully burnt my memory with marijuana, fried my mind with cocaine, LSD, and THC, and then scorched my brain with speed. I washed it all down with my favorite companion, the "king" of beers.

The teachers and staff at Solanco High School in my hometown of Quarryville decided to quietly adjust the curve in their grading system so they wouldn't have to deal with my obnoxious mouth and my corrupt behavior any longer than necessary. They wanted me gone.

"Mr. Nissley," the principal informed me six days before graduation, "I called you in here to tell you that you're not graduating because you made the grades. You're moving on because we don't want you back here next year."

After barely graduating from high school, I went to work as a welder, and one by one I traded in my old friends for new drinking buddies. I needed at least three cases of beer a week to be able to function enough to keep my job. On top of that, I needed several additional cases to keep my friends supplied, so I supplemented my income by midnight burglaries of country stores and gas stations. The liquid courage I found in a can caused me to do many things I would never have done if I had been in my right mind.

Each time I sobered up these vicious things haunted me. The only solution I could think of was to stay drunk, so that's what I did. I went to work drunk and came home to get drunk. My life was one prolonged blurry preoccupation with drunken orgies, bar brawls, and criminal activities. My friends nicknamed me "the Funnel." Needless to say, I was a huge disappointment to my Christian parents.

I had had no intention of becoming such a pain in the neck for my mom and dad. The truth is I didn't have a good reason to rebel. I attended Sunday school classes, learned the expected set of Bible verses, and went to church with my dad, mom, brother, and sister. My happy childhood was spent exploring the simple pleasures of good country living; that is until I decided to follow my friends and not my Christian upbringing. Any godly seeds sown in my heart as a young boy were gobbled up by my decision to allow sin to take over my life.

Something's Not Right and It HURTS!

With disdain, I ignored the warnings and admonitions of friends and relatives about the consequences of my riotous living. Then one day at work I had a crisis. Without warning, 1,200 pounds of compressed cardboard fell on me. The material came down like a wall and buried me, pinning me to the floor of the warehouse. As I dug my way out, I noticed my left foot at my waist and if that wasn't bad enough, I was pretty sure it was bent the wrong way. I looked at the backside of my knee and thought, *This isn't right. Something's very wrong here. I hurt and I have a feeling I'm in big trouble!*

> One day at work 1,200 pounds of compressed cardboard buried me.

In a panic, I grabbed my foot and tried to throw it down thinking it might somehow pop back into place. It didn't. My coworkers rushed me to the hospital where the doctors took x-rays and did tests while my lifeless leg hung limp in an air splint.

"You know, Nissley, you're young, you're agile. You should be able to learn how to walk with a prosthesis easily." The doctor's prognosis was amputation two inches above the knee joint.

My violent temper immediately filled the hospital room. I grabbed a crutch in an attempt to beat the doctor. As I was reaching and swinging, the doctor crawled under the bed and escaped out the door. I managed to grab a handful of syringes and fling them at the fleeing physician. He decided it might be in everyone's best interest if I got a second opinion!

"I hear you are opposed to amputation," a different doctor stated. "There is something else we might try."

It was the only alternative to amputation. I would have to endure a total of nine operations and extensive physical therapy. Surgeries transplanted muscles and removed ligaments and cartilage. Orthopedic surgeons retracted my kneecap and reattached muscles to bones with stainless-steel staples. A custom-made brace helped me walk. They told me it would work for five to seven years, but then the leg would have to come off. There was no way to make it last longer, let alone permanently. But there were some benefits of treatment.

Following Doctor's Orders?

I pushed the call button for the nurse to bring in another bottle of my favorite beer and thought, *This is the life! Room service at its finest!* Although being seriously injured and in the hospital was inconvenient, life was relatively good.

The doctors agreed that I was a special case in that sudden detoxification from alcohol would cause me more harm than good. They thought they were being both practical and merciful when they prescribed a realistic dosage of alcohol—at least a six-pack of beer per day—to make my stay less traumatic. But their primary concern was to avoid the grisly symptoms of alcoholic withdrawal known as the DTs. The doctors' worst fear was that leg spasms would rip open crucial stitches and staples embedded within my severely damaged leg. With my buddies, I devised ways to make life even better. We combined forces and supplemented my prescription with whiskey smuggled in under their jackets and with get well wishes.

After a couple of drunken weeks, I finally left the hospital, returning from time to time for the other eight surgeries. I spent a year and a half on crutches and in physical therapy between trips to the hospital. The only thing I knew to do was to drink a case of beer and half a fifth of tequila every day while collecting Workman's Compensation and Social Security checks. These were the benefits of being labeled permanently disabled, or so I thought.

Then someone told my parents, who had patiently loved me through all of this, that I was abusing heavy drugs, not just alcohol. After two years of waiting on me hand and foot, my parents confronted me, hoping I would come to my senses. It didn't work. They decided to evict their slug of a son.

I thought I had figured out who had ratted on me and decided he deserved a good beating, but when I found him, instead of fighting we talked. Charlie listened as I griped about my pending eviction.

"Just go to church," he told me.

"No way! I'd rather die!" I responded. But after giving it some thought, I decided if I went, at least my parents would get off my back for a while, and I could continue my rent-free living arrangements and have enough funds to support my growing addictions and my obsession with chaos.

A Skeptical Rebel

When sinners go to church they often feel like long-tailed cats in a room full of rocking chairs. This was especially true for me, wild man Denny Nissley, who had committed practically every sin ever invented. Nevertheless, I took a chance and went to a church service in southern Lancaster County. Since this church was in a big barn, it seemed less dangerous than a "real" church.

As soon as I went the first time, the Jesus freaks from the church started getting to me. As I lay in bed at night during the days after that first visit, I tried to figure out what they had that I didn't. They convinced me to

> When sinners go to church they often feel like long-tailed cats in a room full of rocking chairs.

go back a second time, which satisfied and delighted my parents.

On that morning I sat by the back door with my friend Charlie. The preacher did his number and the salvation message began. I had heard it all before, "With every head bowed, every eye closed . . ." I could almost taste the beer that would be going down my funnel right after the service. Then something captured my attention.

"Somebody in here doesn't believe Jesus is real."

I said to myself, *Yeah, Mister, that's me all right. How's he know what I'm thinking?*

"If you don't believe Jesus is real, then why don't you put Him to the test? If you ask Him, He'll make Himself real to you."

Oh, okay, God, if you're up there, and I really don't think you are, I want you to let me know, I prayed. I had a sense that all six feet, one inch, two hundred pounds of me was slowly drifting to the left, towards Charlie. I opened my eyes to see if I was crowding Charlie or not, but my friend wasn't there. I looked around. It wasn't Charlie who had moved, I had. I was standing halfway up the aisle headed towards the front of the barn. This in itself was a miracle since I never intended to respond to anything while in a church service. I was convinced churches were for weaklings and hypocrites.

I felt as if I were on another planet. I was a maximum tough guy, a bouncer at some of the county's rowdiest bars. (Employment I had obtained by thrashing the bar's existing bouncer, throwing him out the door, and finding the manger to ask for his job.) Tough guys who are full of themselves don't usually go to church, let alone respond to an altar call.

Another thing dumbfounded me. In addition to not being able to recall walking down the aisle, the usual throbbing in my leg was missing. In fact, my leg didn't hurt at all. I looked around and it seemed as if everyone was looking at me. Fortunately, others were going forward so I followed them. They knelt down, which was a problem for me since I only had one good knee, but somehow I knelt, too.

The moment I knelt down something supernatural happened. I began to weep. A stockpile of shame surfaced as I let go of years of mental and emotional anguish that had been covered up and numbed by my devoted substance abuse. I couldn't explain the unrestrained tears. I sobbed like a baby. The preacher came over and asked, "What do you want?"

"I don't know," was my muffled reply.

"Do you want Jesus?"

"Yeah, I guess so," I said. The preacher and another man grabbed my hands and prayed as I received Jesus as my Savior in a circle of three. Tears of shame and remorse were instantaneously driven out by an indescribable inner peace.

"I have to sit down," I told them. "I've got a bum knee." They probably thought I had a knee injury from playing football, perhaps a strain or something of that nature.

"Jesus will heal that leg just as He did when He walked on this earth," they informed me. "Would you like us to pray for you?"

"Yeah, sure. Go for it." I figured I'd try anything once.

They finished praying and announced, "You're healed."

"Really?"

"Sure," they said. "Go ahead. Walk. Stand up and try it out!"

I did. I was totally pain free for the first time in two

years. "Wow!" I cried out loud. *Maybe God healed my leg!* I thought. I rolled up my pant leg and took off the brace. It was then that they knew this was not just an "owie." They couldn't help notice the enormous scars that ran up and down my leg. All of a sudden, they realized they had prayed for a bona fide cripple.

> I jumped in the air and ran around the barn.

I started to walk and the leg stayed in the right place, precisely where it was supposed to be. Like an escaped maniac, I freaked out, jumped up in the air, ran around the barn where church was held, jumping over benches in a state of exhilaration.

"Man, what are you all looking at?" I shouted at the crowd. "God just healed my blankety-blank leg!" No one reprimanded me for swearing in church. Instead, shouts of joy went up before the Lord. "Praise God! Hallelujah!" everyone seemed to be saying.

I realized I had finally reached true freedom and that God was real. My notion of a longhaired guru sitting on the top of a mountain with his big stick ready and waiting to clobber sinners was gone. I knew God was not some pie in the sky or special occasion cake, but that He is the Bread of Life, made for everyday use!

Miracle upon miracle, the day I became a born-again believer was the same day I was delivered of drug and alcohol addiction. On the way home, I pulled out my cigarettes, put one in my mouth, pushed in the lighter and thought, *This feels funny here in my mouth. I don't need this anymore!*

I crumpled up the pack of cigarettes and started to throw it out the car window and thought, *Wait a minute. That wouldn't be right. That's God's country out there and I'd be littering.* I threw the trash on the floor instead and thought about how different I felt. With refreshing clarity, I noticed everything had changed.

It became overwhelmingly obvious to everyone who knew me that my ungodly anger, bitterness, racism, and perverted thoughts were gone. A mysterious new affection for people replaced my vicious attitudes, and new habits replaced the unhealthy old ones. My mother, Betty, and my father, Ernie, couldn't have been happier. They could not wait to tell my aunts and uncles and all the folks at church that had been praying for my salvation. Denny Nissley had not only received Christ, but was healed, set free, *and* delivered from drug and alcohol addiction! What great news.

It all happened on April 3, 1977, and it was the most glorious day of my life.

The Evidence Is Proof Positive

Shortly after my conversion, the doctors at Temple University Hospital scheduled an extensive battery of tests for me that would take nearly eight hours to complete. To their amazement, they discovered ligaments and cartilage they had removed had grown back.

Transplanted muscles had returned to their normal locations, and the stainless steel staples they had driven into my bones had vanished. On the Friday before that church service, I measured 15 percent strength in my bum leg. On Monday after the church service, I measured 97 percent strength in my healed leg.

I found out later that my physical therapist was profoundly affected by what had happened to me. He told God that he was going to watch me for thirty days and if the dramatic changes in my life proved to be lasting, then he, too, would serve God. God had to prove that He could mend a shattered life as well as a shattered leg.

I used to think God turned people into freaks. The truth is quite the opposite. He turns freaks like me into productive human beings. If God reached down to shake the barrel, and then scraped it in order to get Denny Nissley out, surely no one is beyond His reach. I'm one of His best examples of unconditional love. God spared my life and saved me, Denny Nissley, the "most likely to die of an overdose" in my high school class of '73. He also called me into full-time ministry. God filled my funnel with streams of Living Water and began to use me to pour out His love to people of all types, especially those least likely to pursue religious contact.

A thousand cases of beer never satisfied my thirst but one taste of Jesus' prescription of Living Water gave me exactly what I needed and much more than I ever dreamed possible. And it came with a lifetime guarantee; a lifetime filled with incredible hope, extraordinary love, innumerable blessings, unparalleled peace, tremendous joy, and a retirement plan good enough to die for.

CHAPTER TWO

Living with Death Threats

Denny has had numerous death threats because of his outspoken faith in God. They began in Dallas, Texas, when he attended Christ for the Nations Institute. He didn't excel academically due to his overwhelming desire to minister to the pimps and prostitutes of downtown Dallas. But some would say he excelled in ministry. The incidents recounted in this chapter convinced Denny that death is not something to be feared.

God called me to Bible school a year and a half after being born again. When I told my friends, they questioned me, "Are you sure, Denny? You can't even spell Bible school!" It was true. I had never studied, not a single day in my godless life. In fact, I couldn't remember attacking even one homework assignment. When I was young, the only reason I carried a book around was in case someone decided to mess with me. I used books to defend myself and to attack any poor soul who challenged me.

Going to Bible school seemed absurd, but I knew it was God's plan for my life. When someone mentioned Christ for the Nations, I decided to go there. I sent a letter, bought a three-piece suit, cut my hair, and moved to Dallas. While a student at Christ for the Nations, I took a small team of a few zealous Bible students to downtown Dallas for street ministry. In my heart, I knew God wanted me to reach out to the prostitutes on Cedar Springs Avenue, a notorious strip. I also felt a burden to reach the pimps. Unfortunately, pimps, hookers, and Bible School students don't keep the same hours, so I had to break a few rules to save a few souls.

I'll be the first to confess my burden for street people affected my better judgment. I frequently stayed out past the 11:00 P.M. curfew on weekends to minister to the perverts, pimps, prostitutes, and anyone else within earshot. I find it intriguing that one of the most important lessons I ever learned happened on the streets, not in the classroom.

Be Still and Know

Evelyn was my street ministry partner. A Puerto Rican from New York, Evelyn stood all of four feet, eleven inches. While a hooker, Evelyn had been saved and discipled at the New Life for Girls program. She proved to be the perfect partner for one particular mission.

It was way past curfew when Evelyn and I came face to face with a disgruntled pimp on a sidewalk. "I don't like you being here," the pimp said. "How 'bout I take your woman here and put her into some white slavery?"

> "Over my dead body."

"Over my dead body," I said courageously. The next thing I knew a long, cold blade was resting on my Adam's apple. I didn't know where it came from or how it got there, but when the cutting edge began to gently press down on my flesh, I stopped wondering and stood still. The pimp looked at me with eyes of steel and said, "That can be arranged." I believed him. It occurred to me that my Bible school teachers had not yet covered what to do when an angry pimp puts a knife to your throat. Was it possible I missed that class?

I stood there while intense fear began to grip and invade my thoughts. *Where did the man with the faith and power for the hour go? It ain't me, God! I'm scared. I'm gonna die, and I'm thinking I don't want to die right now!*

Mr. "How 'Bout I Take Your Woman" decided to press a little harder until a trickle of warm blood ran down my neck. I didn't even have to look. I knew that if I sneezed my Adam's apple was going to get cored, and the only Scripture that came to mind was "Be still and know I am God."

So I stood there paralyzed. I thought, *Oh God, what am I going to do? Lord, this would be a good time for a lightning strike. Why don't you just smite this pest with a bolt?* Actually, in a very short period of time, I compiled a list of twenty different ways God could eradicate the heartless reprobate. Then suddenly out of the blue Evelyn, with her arms flailing, exploded like a bottle rocket.

"Man, you don't know what chou're doin'! Don't chou know who this is, man? This is God's man! This man is God's holy property, man! And chou got a knife stuck on his throat, man! Don't chou know what God could do to you, man?"

I thought, *Woman! Evelyn, you don't know what you're doing! You're going to get me killed! Please, be quiet!*

I had never heard a New York Puerto Rican ex-hooker rant and rave so fast, so hard, so long, so quick, so harsh in all my life. I thought, *This isn't the plan I had in mind, but I guess I don't have a say in it because I'm busy being still—-knowing God.*

She finally shut up but she wasn't finished. She glared at him with her cockiest look, eyes wide open, eyebrows raised up to her hairline, hands on her hips, her ninety-five-pound body poised like a deadly weapon.

The pimp looked at her, then looked at me and pulled the knife away from my throat, folded it back up, put it in his pocket and ran away like a scared rabbit.

"Evelyn! You almost got me killed!"

"Chut up, man. Chou're bleedin'!"

> We thanked God for sparing our lives.

The ministry team of Evelyn and Denny decided at this point the outreach was over. After we thanked God for sparing our lives, I dropped Evelyn off at her dormitory and drove around Dallas in my pickup truck reflecting on the night's events.

Later that night, my roommate, another of the godly Charlies in my life, helped me slip into the dorm unnoticed. Charlie didn't go on the covert outreaches, but he stayed up late so he could let me in after hours. When Charlie looked at me, he felt sorry for the sinners who had to spend another night on the streets with the crazy evangelist. When I looked at Charlie, I saw a pastor in the making. I'd be the one to drag them in; he'd be the one to teach them apologetics or whatever else I was supposed to be learning at Bible school. Charlie and I together were a paradox. Before coming to Christ for the Nations, Charlie had study habits and I had drug and alcohol habits. It occurred to me years later that Charles Barton and I were actually perfect teammates, and it was God who put us together so that we could make a difference in the kingdom of God.

Wrestling with God

As I lay in bed thinking about what had just taken place, I thanked God again for getting rid of the pimp. Then I asked the Lord the precarious question, *God, why didn't you just take him out?*

"Denny, you really don't believe in me."

What?

"You really don't believe in me, not really."

God, I sure do believe in you. Remember me? I'm a Christian! I gave up drugs and alcohol for you. I'm going to Bible School here. I cut my hair for you! I'm preaching your gospel! What do you mean I don't believe in you?

Like a tape recorder in my mind, God took me through the evening's events. All at once I realized my thoughts and desires for the knife-wielding pimp did not line up with God's thoughts and desires. I wanted God to destroy him, and God wanted to save him from an eternity in hell. "You wished that he would die on Cedar Springs Avenue and go to hell because you don't believe in me. You love your life more than you love me. You don't believe me enough to say, *Lord, it's okay with me if you take me out of this world.*"

After wrestling with God for an hour, I felt I had to tell Charlie. "Charlie, wake up. Charlie!"

"What's the matter?"

"Charlie! I don't even believe in God, man!"

"Yes, you do, Denny. You're a Christian!"

"No, I don't. You're lying to me! You're not gonna believe what happened tonight." I tried to explain the impasse. The two of us knelt by the side of the bed and prayed for a good while, then Charlie went to bed. The first glimpse of morning light to enter the dorm room found me still seeking God. During the hours of complete honesty in which I emptied myself before God, I surrendered my life never to take it back again. God wanted me to trust Him with everything. But not only that, He wanted me to trust Him exclusively.

God searched my heart and exposed thoughts and attitudes that I knew were holding me back from pursuing God's will wholeheartedly. I gave up control of every aspect of my life, especially my ministry. I cried out to God to forgive my selfish attitudes. I lamented over my lack of compassion. I begged for cleansing from my heavenly Father. From that day forward I knew God would work through me without being hampered by my selfish desire to live. I had acquired an undeniable, reverential longing to be with God. I was living without the fear of death, but that's not to say I didn't have opportunities to be fearful. In fact, I had several more opportunities to imagine my home going while I was at Bible school.

In Hostile Territory

There was the time I came up with a brilliant plan to rescue a prostitute from her deplorable life on the streets. Shirley had given her life to the Lord, but she and her two-year-old son still lived with her pimp in a housing project in Dallas.

Shirley's situation seemed utterly hopeless. Because she represented income, the pimp literally held her hostage by threatening to kill her little boy if she didn't return home to him. If she didn't bring home

> If she didn't bring home enough money, he'd beat her son.

enough money, he'd beat her son right in front of her, burning his tender young flesh with cigarettes.

I decided to look and act like a heathen in order to pull the wool over her pimp's eyes. I bought the most ungodly clothing I could find at the Salvation Army store, completely aborting the school's dress code. My ingenious strategy was to act as if Shirley and I had plans to go to the Laundromat together. This way Shirley would have her clothes after the rescue. In the getaway car, there would be a Christian girl also dressed in heathen clothes. My character, a typical street-savvy thug, liked hanging out with loose women. The escape plan was perfectly prearranged and everyone was confident it would play out like a scene from an action movie.

"Hey, dude, got a smoke?" I asked her pimp. A cigarette came flying through the air. I caught it and popped it in my mouth, letting it hang there loosely.

"Stupid lazy broad's been buggin' me all day. Now I gotta take her to the Laundromat. It's always something." I was making casual conversation with the pimp while Shirley and her son were stuffing their belongings into a garbage bag. As they were shuffling their way to the door, I tossed the cigarette back to him.

"Yeah, I know what you mean," he said, catching the cancer stick.

Suddenly, the girl in the car cried out, "Hey, what's taking so long? We gotta get outa here!" The "hostages" went first, and when I got one foot out the door, the pimp abruptly woke up.

"Hey, wait a minute," he said anxiously. "She just did the laundry yesterday!"

"Oh, geez," I said frantically thinking of something to say. "That ain't none of my business."

"Something's not right here."

I thought, *How about that? This guy's a prophet! What in the world was she thinking doing her laundry the day before the rescue?* Apparently, cleanliness is next to godliness. We took a few steps forward away from the apartment.

"You take another step and you're dead," the pimp informed me.

I turned around and said, "You're right, buddy. You've been had. I'm a preacher and she's a Christian. Your girl done gave her life to God and she's gonna live for Jesus now." I said this to a guy with a gun pointed at my head. "Shirley's leaving, man. We're taking her and her son outta here."

I turned and faced the getaway car.

"No," came the reply.

Both women looked at me wondering what to do next. I shouted, "Get in the car with the boy, ladies!"

"Denny! He'll kill you! He will kill you, Denny!"

"Don't worry about me! Get in the car! Just get in the car!" I took another step, which brought about another menacing death threat. "You take one more step and I'll kill you!"

I took another step.

"No, I don't think you will. You see, it's not worth it, you pulling the trigger. If you pull the trigger and I die, you're gonna rot in prison for at least twenty years and I'm going to heaven. Then you're gonna rot in hell because you killed someone and I'll still be in heaven. How do I know this? If you've noticed, my voice is at a very loud pitch right now, and because my voice is so loud, all your neighbors are looking out their windows to see what's going on here. They've seen you with a gun to my head, and now we have plenty of eyewitnesses to send you to prison. No problem, man. You won't have the hooker, I'll be in heaven, and you'll be on your way to jail. Is that what you want?"

The pimp didn't say it out loud, but I could hear him thinking, *Oh, man, this guy's right. What do I do now?*

I continued, "Listen, I don't want you gettin' jittery, but I am leaving now and if you have a brain in your head, you won't shoot me. But if you do, I want you to know I'm going to heaven. Now, here I go. I'm gonna move my left foot."

"You take that step and you're a dead man!"

I took two steps.

"You take another step and I'll kill you!" Six steps later I heard, "You take any more steps and I'll kill you! You touch that car door and I'll kill you! You open that car door, and you're a dead man! Get out of that car, man, or I'll kill you! If you start that car, you're a dead man! Turn it off, or I'll kill you! Put it back in park, man, or I'll kill you! Get back in this driveway! You're a dead man!"

No one died and never once did I think, *God, take him out.*

The Real Thing

Another disgruntled pimp hired a professional hitman to kill me, but I didn't realize it until one night a very well-dressed man stopped me on the street. I had a feeling I might be looking at trouble.

"What's wrong?" I asked him.

"You Denny Nissley?" he asked.

"Yeah, that's me." I pulled him off to the side of a darkened alley.

He pulled back one side of his jacket to reveal a huge wad of cash. "I was just paid three thousand dollars."

My first thought was, *I'd like to have your problems.*
Then he opened the other side of his jacket to reveal his shiny 9mm Beretta gun

". . . to kill you," he added.

Apparently, I was reaching
them. *Praise God, I'm reaching too
many Cedar Springs Avenue hook-
ers!* Then I realized I was staring at a real hitman and
there was an actual price on my head. My short-lived
victorious thought quickly became *That's nice, but suddenly I'm very scared.* Although at first I feared for my
life, the peace and security of knowing God's precious
promises came flooding in, overtaking the enemy's
empty threats against my life. "Have you prayed about
this?" I asked out of the blue.

"What? What did you say to me?" he asked in
amazement.

"I said, did you pray about whether or not you
should kill me? If you're gonna kill one of God's ser-
vants, don't you think you'd better ask God first before
you do it?"

It came stumbling out, "Well, I, ah, ah, well, yeah,
maybe. I guess maybe I should."

"You'd better. Think about it. This is serious stuff
here. You know how to find me, right? You can kill me
any day, isn't that right?"

"Yeah, that's right. Gordon Lindsey Hall, Room
211, preacher man Denny Nissley," he said, making

sure I knew that he also knew my name. When he was done letting me see his gun, he walked away.

I fell to the ground on my knees. "Thank you, Lord. You've spared my life. Now spare his, Lord. Save his soul and let the light of your grace shine tonight, Lord. When he prays, dear God, help him to find Jesus."

Four days later, the pimp found me on the streets. He did not look happy. "Kenneth gave back the money!" he said, annoyed.

Two things were confirmed. Hitman had a name, and it was the disgruntled pimp who wanted me dead. "So, it was you," I said.

"Yeah, so it was. Man, you're lucky. I've seen Kenneth kill somebody for twenty-five dollars! But I figured it out. If I mess with you, I mess with God, so I called off the hit."

A couple of days later, I ran into Kenneth on the streets. He gave me an interesting account of what took place shortly after he decided not to kill me. "I prayed like you told me to, Denny. On my knees by my bed cause that's the way I figured it's done. But nothing happened. I think I fell asleep."

"Oh," I said. I thought, *That's good news. At least he took my advice.*

"But the next day I saw this guy handing out little pieces of paper at the store, ya know, whadda ya call 'em? Gospel tracts? Anyway, I asked if he knew you. I figured anyone handing out gospel tracts had to know you. He said he didn't know you. I couldn't believe it.

Anyway, he did say he knew Jesus, and that was what really mattered. He told me I could give my life to God and that he would pray for me. So, I prayed again. I prayed with the guy right there and God saved me! Can you believe that? I'm one of yous now!" he said with open excitement.

"Praise God. Thank you Jesus!" We shouted and rejoiced together.

"Hey, come here, man," I said pulling him off to the same alley where we'd had our last conversation. "God saved you and now He's gonna fill you with His Holy Ghost."

"What? Fill me? Fill me with what?"

"Shut up, man. You gonna love it!"

I laid hands on the ex-hitman and God filled him with the Holy Spirit. No church service or Sunday school, no how-to seminar, just the laying on of hands and the prayers of a Bible school student who had a burden for street people. It's not recorded anywhere or taught in any Bible school, but a revival took place in an alley by a dumpster in Dallas. I had uncovered holy ground on a side street.

> I laid hands on the ex-hitman and God filled him with the Holy Spirit.

Afterward, I once again fell to my knees to pour out my gratitude to God for not only sparing my life but for letting me experience the answer to my prayer. What a thrill it was to witness a soul being snatched from the very depths of darkness! It wasn't just any ordinary soul. It was someone paid in advance to exterminate me, the pesky street preacher.

Can't Quit and Won't Die

"You Denny, ain't cha?" the man said in a seriously distinguishable, twangy, Texan accent. Not everyone in the downtown Dallas red light district knew me by name, but most of them had heard about me. I was their resident street preacher. I made no attempt to hide the fact I had come to preach the gospel, but what they didn't realize was that I was the leader of a gang of Bible school radicals bent on destroying their businesses.

One particular "nude modeling" place got thumped on pretty hard by the Holy Ghost hitmen from Christ for the Nations. The seedy business charged people twenty dollars to watch twenty minutes of nude modeling. MasterCard and VISA were accepted, but that wasn't satisfactory for us zealous Christians. We were determined not to stop until Jesus was accepted, too. It was a legitimate business in Dallas but not in the eyes of God.

"You that street preacher everyone's talkin' bout, ain't cha?" the Texan asked.

"That's right. I'm Denny. And you are—?"

"I'm Kerry. I manage this place. Someone told me they saw you prayin' over my buildin'. Whatcha trying to do, get the buildin' saved?" he asked. He seemed pleased with himself, standing there letting the brim of his faded cowboy hat shade his tanned, thin face.

"No, Kerry, we laid our hands on the building and cursed your business," I said.

"Well, I didn't think Christians were supposed to cuss," he chuckled.

"You don't understand. I said we cursed your business. That means we asked God to make it go bankrupt so you'd have to go out, get a job, and work by the sweat of your brow like the Bible says. And we asked God to let these women who work to satisfy the lusts of sinful men come out from their slavery and accept Jesus as their Savior so they can live for Him."

"Hmmm. I don't like thaa . . . aat," he said thoughtfully.

"Well, I didn't think you woo . . . uuld," I informed him.

Kerry reached backward into the corner of his raunchy office, grabbed a 12-gauge, double-barrel, sawed-off shotgun, put two shells in it, and

> He pulled the triggers and again the hammers would not release.

planted himself between the door and me. With the gun to my ear, he cocked the hammers and started to pull back on the triggers. I could see Kerry's fingers turning red. The gun was shaking he was pulling so hard. Kerry stared at me and withdrew the gun. He checked the safety, pushing it through the other way, and then pointed the gun at my head again. He pulled the triggers and again the hammers would not release. He was speechless, gazing at me in amazement.

Since there was a standoff going on between him and God, I decided to sing, "The weapons of our warfare are not carnal, but they are mighty in the Holy Ghost. . . ."

Kerry looked at me as if I was crazy. "You're nuts! You're about to die and you're singing Sunday school hymns!"

"Yeah, but I'm not dead now, am I? Look at me! I'm alive!" This time I had the cocky smile.

Kerry put the gun down in defeat. He thought for a moment and said, "Thanks, Denny. Thanks for praying for my business. Ever since you prayed, my business has been doin' real goo-ood."

"Yeah, but now that you know, it's going under," I said emphatically. I got up and left Kerry alone so he might consider what had just happened.

It was Saturday night, the busiest night of the week, so I decided to observe the booming business by going back in and sitting on a couch in the reception area. When a customer sat down beside me, I asked innocently, "Hey, how ya doin'? You come here often?" Before he could answer I started telling him about Jesus.

"What happened, this place become a church?" he asked.

"No, not yet," I laughed.

Kerry was livid but extremely curious to find out what made me so bold. He and his girlfriend, who happened to be one of the strippers, decided they'd take the street preacher, the intended murder victim, out for some steak and eggs.

"Hold it! You don't know what they did to this food." I stopped them from gobbling down the grub. "Better let a man of God pray over it," I suggested.

"Well, when you put it that way," Kerry's girlfriend said softly. They looked at each other in a somewhat mesmerized state. I prayed and then shared my testimony. The two irreligious people listened as I tried to show them how to make things between them and God all right.

The day after the failed murder attempt Kerry took his shotgun out to the country where he shot round after round after round. Apparently, the safety on this particular gun wasn't even working. There was no doubt in Kerry's mind that my brains should have been blown apart the day before. He knew there was no earthly explanation as to why the gun would not go off just the day before.

The next time Kerry saw me he asked, "Hey, Denny, remember the other night? Whaa . . . att do you think happened?" I conveyed what I could about the power of God and Kerry listened, probably out of respect.

We cautiously developed a friendship over the next few months. I took Kerry to the gym where we played basketball, lifted weights, and went swimming. When the right time came, Kerry accepted my invitation to go to church. He brought his girlfriend, and she brought their little boy. I had to break a few Bible school rules and give up some personal time, but it was worth it because a pervert became a saint and so did his girlfriend, who later became his wife. Kerry got out of the "nude modeling" business and found a real job somewhere.

I was more determined than ever to take the love of Jesus to where it was most desperately needed and hardest to find. During my time at Christ for the Nations, I became a God-fearing, devil-hating, Holy Ghost hitman whose heart's desire was to faithfully execute orders from headquarters: "Go out into the highways and hedges, and compel the people to come in." In my case, that meant going into the strip joints of Dallas, Texas. It was that plain and that simple.

Holy Ghost Hitmen

Professional hitmen don't normally travel in packs, but during the late seventies the righteous ones in Dallas did. It wasn't long before the other managers who followed Kerry in the "nude modeling" business got saved and the business had to close its doors. A similar business tried to open in its place, but there were too many sacred strikes by the Holy Ghost hitmen, the Bible school students from Christ for the Nations. Again, the business went under.

When the owner of the building got wind of what was going on, he decided to call the street preacher himself. "Hey, you Denny Nissley, that street preacher guy?"

"Yeah, I'm Denny and I've been known to preach on some streets."

"Listen, I gotta know more about this God you've been preaching about." He sounded distressed.

"Okay, where should we meet?" I asked. I thought I was making an appointment to counsel someone in need.

"How about that old strip joint, ya know, 'Live Nude Models'?"

I was about to meet Ron, the owner of the building. I found out later that Ron had another vocation. He was the leader of the Dallas chapter of the Hell's Angels biker gang. Meanwhile, I was thrilled at the prospect of ministering to a potential convert. It seemed miraculous that God was doing such great and mighty works on the boulevard. I felt privileged and honored to play a part in this phenomenal move of the Holy Spirit.

The door flung open. "I'm Ron. Come on in, preacher," he said slowly. As he stared at me, I couldn't help notice his beady eyes appeared to have muscles of their own. In his case, looks alone could have killed. It was plain to see he wasn't thrilled about leaving behind whatever sins he had been committing to come hear a sermon. I realized by the looks of things, he had no intention of receiving any counseling. I went in anyway. Ron shut the door behind him and locked it with a key, which he threw down on a beat-up old coffee table. I sat on the worn-out sofa while the biker wrapped himself around a chair he had turned around. He totally looked and acted the part: Murderer, First degree.

"Preach to me mister. And you'd better make it good 'cause it'll be your last sermon." Much to my surprise, Ron was not the only one in the audience. The devil showed up to let me know he was there to listen in on my session with his disciple. I was surrounded by fear until I realized there was one more person in attendance. God assured me He was right there beside me.

> "You'd better make it good 'cause it'll be your last sermon."

So I preached the Bible "from Genesis to Maps" (all the way at the back of the Bible). I told Ron everything I ever knew, heard of, or thought about God and ended by saying, "Now mister, what do you think?"

"Are you done?" Ron asked in a serious tone.

"Yeah," I said. "I'm done."

All the time I was preaching, I looked for Ron's weapon. He wasn't wearing a jacket, so a gun or a knife would have been hard to hide. I kept thinking, *How's this guy gonna kill me?* I had forgotten that the place came equipped with a German Shepherd attack dog with size extra-large teeth.

Ron called for the dog and from a back room somewhere the dog came charging at full speed down the long corridor.

I looked at Ron straight in the eyes, pointed to the dog, addressed the devil, and shouted, "Be still in the name of Jesus!" All of a sudden, everything became still. Only the dog's whimpering interrupted the holy silence. The dog had withdrawn and laid down about twenty-five feet from where I was standing.

"All right mister," I challenged him one last time. "You've heard the word of God, you've seen the power of God. It's heaven or hell. Either you turn, or you burn! What'll it be?"

Ron looked at his impotent dog, unlocked the door, and cursed at me as I slowly approached the exit. When we were eyeball to eyeball, nose to nose, he let out a gnarly growl. "Get out!"

I left unharmed, but the devil took quite a beating.

CHAPTER THREE

Keeping Divine Appointments

The stories in this chapter depict the crucial turning points in Denny's life after Bible school that helped shape his commitment to follow the leading of the Holy Spirit no matter what. As he obeys, Denny fulfills his spiritual destiny and many of the seemingly random happenings of his life turn into divine appointments. Denny lets God be in charge.

In Denny's weakness God's strength can be manifested. If Denny does something extraordinary for God, it's not because he has some great talent or wonderful self-esteem; it's simply because God is able to work through him. He often tells people since they have to trust their taxes to the mud-slinging politicians, they ought to trust their lives to the blood-slinging King of kings. That's his credo, and that's precisely why amazing things never stop happening.

I was eating with a friend in a restaurant in Greeley, Colorado, when God laid it on my heart to stand up and preach. I argued with God, telling Him, *Lord, you've got to be nuts!*

Nevertheless, I preached, and everyone stopped what he or she was doing. I mean everyone. The dishwasher stopped washing dishes. The manager stopped managing. The customers stopped eating. The mashed potatoes got cold and the ice cream melted.

Once the manager got over the shock of having a stray street preacher inside his restaurant, he walked toward me as if he was going to take control. I looked at him, pointed my finger, and I said, "Hold on, I'm not finished." Unfortunately for the restaurant manager, I hadn't had an altar call yet.

"Folks, if you're in here and you don't believe what I'm saying, you ask God and He'll make Himself real to you."

A man stood up and said, "Preacher, I've got a bad back. What's your God gonna do about that?"

Instantly, I was drenched with the power of God. "Sir, God told me your one leg's too short. Now sit down," I instructed the skeptic.

"Are you his wife?" I asked the woman next to him.

"Well, yes," she answered not knowing what else to do.

"Come here. Hold his legs up." She did exactly what I said.

"See that?" I exclaimed. "One of your legs is at least

a couple of inches too short!" By this time everyone in the restaurant wanted to see this poor man's short leg.

After the crowd had gathered around, I gently laid my hand on her shoulder, not his, and prayed. The customers, the dishwasher, and the manager all witnessed the man's leg grow. His wife thought she was hallucinating and dropped his legs.

> The customers, the dishwasher, and the manager all witnessed the man's leg grow.

The man stood up and shouted, "I'm healed!" It was obvious to everyone he was healed because his one pant leg was noticeably too short!

I asked his wife, "Ma'am, why is his one pant leg too short?"

She stuttered in disbelief, "I guess, preacher, because, I, ah, I hemmed it up because his one leg used to be too short!"

"Is that right?" I asked.

That day one man gave his life to the Lord, a woman rededicated her life to the Lord and got baptized in the Holy Ghost, and another woman asked me to pray for her because she had bursitis and arthritis. We prayed all right. We had "church-itis" that night, right there in the restaurant in Greeley because I let God be in charge.

But when I went home that night I had a visitor. The devil invaded my victory party to tell me I was a jerk. "You might as well pack your bags and leave town.

You're gonna be labeled a nutcase. What are you doing preaching in a public place? You fool! Nobody's going to let you come minister at their church," the devil tormented me. I felt as if I was beneath the valley, which was bizarre because I had just come from such a glorious mountaintop. I desperately sought God, *Where are You? How come I feel so rotten?* And then I heard God's voice tenderly speaking to my heart.

"Go ask that man that was healed if he thinks you're a jerk, Denny. Ask the man whose sins were forgiven today if he thinks you're a jerk. Ask the woman who got filled with My Spirit if she thinks you ought to pack your bags and leave town. Ask me on Judgment Day what I think about your obedience."

Eat or Pray

Then there was a different restaurant in another state. I came out from the restroom and right there in front of me was a man having an epileptic seizure. He was convulsing, so I grabbed him by the waist and started praying. "God heal this man. Take your hands off this man, devil! Let him alone! Be healed in Jesus' name!" I didn't make any attempt to restrain my voice and purposely kept my eyes closed. I didn't want to see what might have been going on around me.

All of a sudden, I felt a big, cumbersome hand on my shoulder and thought, *Oh, good. I've got some agreement going on here.* So I kept praying until I felt the man had been released, and when I opened my eyes, I knew God had touched him.

"Are you all right?" I asked the man.

"Yes, I am. Thanks," he replied.

I looked over my shoulder and saw the owner of the big arm I had felt earlier. "Hi, there. Are you a Christian?" I asked.

"I'm the manager," answered the man in an unfriendly tone.

"Ah-huh," I knew there would be more in this declaration.

"You can't pray in my restaurant," he informed me.

"What?" I couldn't believe his reaction. It was plain to see the man having the seizure was glad I had prayed. "He was having . . ." I tried to inject a statement.

"I don't care what he was having. You don't pray in my restaurant. It's a restaurant not a church."

"What? God just helped this man!" I thought for a moment and said, "Okay, then, let's suppose you're having a heart attack and you've got two breaths left in you and here come the paramedics. They've backed up the ambulance to the door and they're bringing in all the equipment. I suppose you would want me to tell them, 'Stop! This isn't a hospital; it's a restaurant!'"

The way he glared at me I thought I might be going to the hospital later, but I continued anyway.

"You know, mister manager, you're right. But I don't want anyone to die because this is a restaurant not a church. And for your information, I am the church because where I go, Jesus goes."

"Don't pray in my restau- **"Don't eat** rant" was all he could say. **in church."**

"Fine," I said. "Don't eat in church."

Flying Nuns

I'm energized when God puts me with Christians who are completely submitted to God and sold out for the sake of the kingdom. I truly feel sorry for Christians who haven't relinquished it all. They don't know what they're missing but I do because I've seen what happens when God is in charge.

Four friends and I were strolling around the Arch and the museum area in St. Louis, Missouri, when I spotted a group of nuns. I've always admired nuns for their godly devotion, so we stopped to talk to the sisters. We engaged in a friendly conversation about the majesty of God. They appeared to be interested in what we do so we told them about our upcoming outreach to their local community event. After a while other people stopped to listen, and before long we were having church. At the time it seemed appropriate for our group to join together for a word of prayer. As we and the nuns formed a snug circle, a man from the streets saw us huddled up for prayer and asked if he could join us. When this man started praying, the glory of God came on all of us. We were immersed in God's love, and for fifteen minutes we experienced heaven on earth, all of us kids just talking to Dad, our heavenly Father.

We opened our eyes to find a crowd of curious people had gathered, and where there's a crowd, there ought to be a preacher. I couldn't help myself. I had to preach, especially after the rip-snorting prayer meeting we had just had. The nuns looked as if they were about to fly away! They had never been in a charismatic meeting. "I wish the power of God would take over our prayer meetings as it has the streets of St. Louis!" one sister confided. The nuns continued to watch in awe as God ministered to people on the streets. We weren't even near a church!

I thought it was interesting that the man from the streets, who could easily be mistaken for a bum, had prayed with so much power and might. He turned out to be someone I met in Dallas while I attended Christ for the Nations. Brother Matthew had a long history of winning to Christ at least three people a day, not from a pulpit but on the streets. During that day I rediscovered that when God is given complete control, His accomplishments and results far exceed what we can achieve without Him. The Bible says we can do nothing apart from Him. And I like to say, apart from Him, we should do nothing!

A Turning Point

The importance of doing the Lord's will was reinforced

for me early one afternoon on a trip in the Southwest. My wife and I, only recently married, pulled up to a convenience store on the outskirts of the city where I was scheduled to preach later that night. Two teenage boys were in the middle of a boisterous fistfight. People stood around gasping as the Anglo and Mexican teens locked horns. The two were having it out tooth and nail, both bent on winning.

I shoved the gearshift into park and told Sandy, "I feel as if the Lord told me to preach to break up the fight."

"Well, Denny?" she said matter-of-factly.

I jumped out of the van and started towards the boys just as

> The Lord told me to preach.

another man stepped out from the crowd and successfully pulled the boys apart and broke up the fight.

"Go home, everyone. This is over," the man informed the crowd.

I got back in the van and Sandy looked at me funny and said, "Didn't you say the Lord told you to preach?"

I thought about my wife's question and immediately began to rationalize my excuse. "Well, it was just to break up the fight and now there's nothing to break up."

"Oh," Sandy continued. "I thought that if the Lord told you to preach, He might have wanted you to preach." I felt convicted but not for long. There was nothing I could do. There was no one left to preach to, so we left.

Sandy and I were getting ready to order our meal at a restaurant later that evening when we discovered our waitress had been crying. Her puffy eyes and the expression on her face exposed her sorrow, so I told her I was a minister and offered my support.

"Oh, praise the Lord; I'm a Christian. It's my nephew. A Mexican boy shot and killed my nephew today. The two of them were in a fight at a convenience store, and after that things went from bad to worse."

Our ears perked up, my throat began to go shut, and my eyes started to well up with tears. Sandy and I knew what she was about to tell us. I reached out to grab ahold of my wife's hand.

"After the fight, the Mexican boy found my nephew at the edge of town, got a gun, and shot him to death. It's so terribly sad." She looked at me curiously because at this point it was obvious I was deeply affected by what she was saying. She stared at me as if to say, *There, there, Preacher. It'll be all right. I'm going to be okay.* There wasn't much we could say or do.

I didn't know how deeply I was affected until my anguish came out when I was scheduled to preach that night. Out of my heartache, I told the congregation about the teenager who died, perhaps because I didn't obey God. "I was there, and I felt as if God told me to preach to break up the fight, but I didn't because somebody else broke up the fight. Only God knows what would have happened if I had preached! Please don't misunderstand. I know God hasn't given up His throne to me. I know God is quite capable of saving lives and souls and accomplishing His will without my help. Nevertheless, at that moment I knew beyond any doubt that obedience would be required on a moment to moment basis in God's distinct plan for my life."

The Lord used that senseless tragedy as a turning point in my ministry. Many times since that day, when I have received a prompting from God to do something, if I think, *Naw, I don't feel like it,* I immediately remember the boy who died.

> Whenever I start thinking, *I don't feel like it,* I remember the boy who died.

Afterglow Fellowship

I will not forget that ministry trip for other reasons as well. Another unorthodox event took place in that same town during that same time due to the fact Jonathan Gainsbrugh, a fellow evangelist, and I were scheduled to preach at the same church at the same time. I was told it was because of a clerical oversight, but I know better. God doesn't make mistakes.

It was the Sunday evening service at the Ninety-First Psalm Church, and we decided it was Jonathan's turn to preach. Near the end of his message he turned to me and said, "Brother Nissley. You know what I'm thinking?" He paused. "I'm thinking I'm pretty thirsty after having preached and everything. You thirsty, Brother?"

I didn't know exactly where he was going with this, but I knew I should say yes. "Ya know, Brother Gainsbrugh, I do believe I am thirsty now that you mention it and all."

"Well, maybe we oughta go get a drink after service," Jonathan said casually.

It dawned on me. I knew where he was going, and I knew where I was going after church. "Yes, sir. Might I suggest we go out after service for some afterglow fellowship?" I said without much emotion. About two hundred people sat in the congregation listening in on our conversation.

"Yeah, that's it! That's what I had in mind, Brother Nissley! Anybody interested in joining Brother Denny and me for a little afterglow fellowship? I saw Sonny's Bar and Grille down the road a ways. How 'bout we go there and get us a cold one?"

"That's fine with me, Brother Gainsbrugh. Let's go on and do that," I started to sound a bit more enthused. The people looked at each other. No one knew quite what to say. Perhaps they were thinking, *Oops! These traveling evangelists aren't what we expected!*

Jonathan asked the congregation, "How many want to go to a bar with Brother Denny and me?"

Nobody said or did anything, so I stepped up to the pulpit. "Aw, Brother Jonathan, look, no one wants to go with us. They don't want to win this city for Jesus! They just wanna hear about it. It doesn't look as if they want to evangelize a whole bar, at least not tonight!"

"Okay, folks. I'll tell ya what," Jonathan explained. "Brother Denny and I are going to go. We're going to have a drink at Sonny's. We'll go and make a stand for the Lord down at Sonny's. How many of you want to come along?"

Some folks got the gist of what was developing. Eight people raised their hands when the pastor spoke out. "No way. There's no way! We're not going down to Sonny's Bar and Grille and try to make a stand for Jesus with ten people from my church. We ain't gonna do that! You wanna make a stand for Jesus, Brother Gainsbrugh, you're gonna have to take a whole lot more of us! I'm going with you! Anyone else want to get past the humdrum boring part of your Christian faith?"

"I got kids; I can't go," someone called out.

"My husband and I will stay behind and watch the kids in the nursery!" someone else yelled. Except for the nursery workers and the children, all two hundred church members went to Sonny's for a drink.

> Two hundred church members went out for a drink.

I gave the instructions. "Listen up. It's a drinking establishment; therefore we're going to be paying customers. Just order a Coke or something and don't hesitate to leave the waitress a tip. Don't worry; you'll figure out what to do when we get there. Smile. Smile a lot. Don't preach. Don't pass out tracts. Don't do anything unless you get the word from us."

God in the Pub

I went in and talked to the owner when we arrived. "Listen," I told her, "there's a whole bunch of us out here and we're real thirsty. We were wondering if we could come in and have a drink. The only thing is, as I said, there's a mess of us out here."

She looked delighted. "Sure thing, but we don't have any waitresses on duty except one and the barmaid and myself."

"We could go to the bar and get our own drinks, if that's all right."

"Oh, okay," she said.

I went outside and gave the orders. "All right, now, listen up. They don't have waitresses so trickle up to the bar and get yourself a drink."

The pastor and the church secretary led the procession and were among the first to cautiously enter the cocktail lounge. The rest of the dehydrated congregation filed in after them. Three women at the bar, startled by the oncoming entourage, were more stunned when they saw not only their pastor but also their whole church coming in. One woman grabbed the secretary and whispered in her ear, "Lola, call us tomorrow. We'll get right with God!" With that, the wayward church women slipped out the back door.

It was a grand time of fellowship, everyone sipping Cokes among Sonny's usual forty or so Sunday night customers. No one suspected a church group had infiltrated the local hangout. Jonathan put his two fingers in his mouth and let out a country whistle. "Hey, everyone! I want you all to sing Happy Birthday to my friend Denny."

It wasn't my birthday, and Jonathan didn't say it was. He just asked everyone to sing, and the drunks happily agreed. I played along. "Oh, golly, stop it. You're embarrassing me."

After the song Jonathan started in with, "Speech! Speech! Let's hear from the birthday boy! How 'bout it Denny?"

"Oh, no, no. You guys! What in the world should I say?" I asked, knowing exactly what I was going to say. "Oh, okay. Thank you so much. I guess I should tell you about another birthday I had that was more important than any other day in my life. So I'll tell you about it because I haven't been the same since that day. It was the day I was born again. I was born again not long after my life was spared. Twelve hundred pounds of compressed cardboard fell on my leg. The doctors wanted to amputate. Then in 1977, I let someone talk me into going to a church service." I preached a bit until the crowd caught on and got angry.

"Shut up, man! Give it a rest! No preaching!" The barmaid shouted, "Hey, cut it out! I'm Jewish!"

I turned around, looked at her, and said, "So was Jesus! And he died for the Jews and the Greeks alike!"

The roar of the crowd was getting louder until Jonathan started singing, "God's not dead; He is alive! NO, NO, NO! God's not dead!" It wasn't long until the whole church joined in. An irate man started pumping the jukebox full of quarters and turned the volume way up to drown us out, but a bunch of brothers gathered around the jukebox and sang their hearts out: "God's not dead; He is alive! NO, NO, NO! God's not dead!"

Jonathan and I retreated towards the back door to watch the action. The Christians were singing and dancing and clapping. The majority at Sonny's was having a good time. The minority looked either confused, angry, or intrigued. Jonathan and I looked at each other and suddenly realized we had successfully launched an entire church into bar evangelism.

Just then the back door opened and a policeman walked in. He looked at Jonathan and asked, "What's going on here?"

Jonathan took a sip of his Coke and said, "Well, sir, I'm not sure but it looks to me as though they're having church."

"Aw, for crying out loud. All right, who's in charge here?" the policeman asked in a loud voice.

"Personally, officer" Jonathan looked around, took another sip, and said, "I think I'd have to say it's the Holy Spirit."

"The Holy Ghost's in charge."

The policeman knew he wasn't getting anywhere with Jonathan, so he turned, put his finger on my chest, and said, "You! Come with me." I obeyed.

"What's going on here?" he asked me after we were outside.

"I'm not sure, but I think those people in there are having church," I answered politely.

"Yeah, I heard that. But I gotta know who's in charge, and don't tell me the Holy Spirit's in charge!"

"Well, sir, I gotta be honest with you, whatever He's not in charge of, I don't want any part of!" I added.

He looked at me with his head cocked sideways. "You're in charge, aren't you?"

"No, sir. It's not me. Look around. I'm not in charge." I looked out across the parking lot. There were a half-dozen squad cars parked facing the bar. Officers in riot gear holding shotguns were waiting for orders from their commander. Someone must have called the police station to report a riot.

"You'd better stop them," he said.

"Hey, I'm not in charge! How am I going to stop all those people from singing and having a good time?"

"I'm telling you, we'll go in there and get them out one at a time if you don't do something," the police officer threatened.

About that time, a few guys from the church walked out the back door. One of them worked at the police station.

"Hey, Joe! Come here! What's going on in there?" the frustrated police officer asked his colleague.

"Oh, hey, Sergeant. We're just having fun," Joe replied.

"You're with them?" he asked.

"Yeah."

The sergeant pointed to me and said, "Tell this guy to call them off."

"Look, I think you'd better handle this yourself," Joe said.

"Come on, Joe, help us out here. We can't, ah, we don't know what to do," the sergeant pleaded with his fellow officer.

He sounded desperate, so I stepped in. "Don't worry, we'll go. We were having a little afterglow fellowship but we're done." I got everyone's attention and told the crowd, "We've been asked by the police to leave, so everyone go on home now."

> "Just a little afterglow fellowship, officer."

The church people humbly left the bar, repeating the chorus softly under their breath as the riot police held the door open. For some reason when the congregation saw the police cars in the parking lot, everyone suddenly got enthusiastic about bar evangelism.

"Now what, Brother Denny? Where to?" they asked with excitement outside the bar.

"We're done," I told them. "Go on home."

The pastor, associate pastor, Jonathan, and I were about to leave when the owner came running out the door. "Wait! Pastor! Um, we need you to come back inside." We went back in to discover the waitress and the barmaid standing there, their hands dripping with money. "Your people left this laying on the tables," the waitress said.

"That's a tip," the pastor explained. "They wanted to bless you. They love you, and that's your tip."

"We don't want their money," the barmaid said. The atmosphere had changed. Guilt filled the air. "It's theirs, not ours," the barmaid said.

"No, God loves you and if they left it, He wants you to have it."

The waitress spoke next. "We can't keep it. Would you take it and put it in the offering?"

"I'll tell you what," the pastor said. "Why don't you come to church, and you can put it in the offering? We can't touch that money; it's yours."

As we were leaving, the sergeant followed us to ask, "Where you going from here? Are you going downtown? Tell me which bar." I tried to tell him we were done but he didn't believe me. "Look, we just want to know so we can be prepared, that's all," he pleaded.

"Good night, Sergeant."

The next day the church phone rang off the hook with calls from church members looking to find out the date, time, and location of the next afterglow fellowship.

God's Special Forces

A former Hollywood pimp and Green Beret, the pastor at the Ninety-First Psalm Church, had new orders from

Headquarters. After our night of bar evangelism, he was ablaze with a desire to reach his city for Christ. The following Sunday he asked his congregation, "How many of you want to have an impact on this city for God?"

A scattering of voices cried out.

"How many of you would be willing to quit your job to have an impact on this city? Stand up if you're willing to say, 'as of today, I'm quitting my job so I can minister full-time for one full year to change this city for God.' Stand up right where you are. Who among us can trust God to supernaturally meet their needs for one year?"

> Twelve more workers join the kingdom.

Twelve men stood up. Twelve guys quit their jobs that Sunday to go into the ministry, and that's how the pastor started his evangelism program called God's Special Forces.

"Here's what we're going to do. You men who stood up, you're going to come to this church for six days of prayer. You'll also be fasting. We're all going to fast and pray, and you'll be memorizing chapters from the Word of God. For those of you who didn't or couldn't stand up, we're going to ask you to double and triple your tithe. We're going to give these men their salaries through the church. The people in this church are going to pay these men to make a stand for Jesus in this city."

People all over the congregation stood up to say, "I'll do it," or "I have X number of dollars set aside. We were going to get a new car but as of tonight, that money goes to God's Special Forces! We'll keep our old jalopy for one more year!" In one day, they raised enough money to put twelve men into full-time ministry in their hometown.

When the year was over, every human being in that city had heard the gospel to the point where residents posted signs on their doors that read, "No 91st Psalmers, Jehovah's Witnesses, or Mormons!" God got top billing, of course, because He was in charge.

Daddy's Girls

Jesus can work through children as well as adults. The Bible says about children: "Blessed is the man whose quiver is full of them. They will not be put to shame when they contend with their enemies in the gate" Psalm 127:5. To date, Sandy and I have ten children. Christian children grow up to become great warriors for the Lord. While they grow, the children learn to follow God's leading just like Mom and Dad. Many times children are the most effective at spreading God's love to people. Our children share the gospel without hesitation and are often instrumental when it comes to taking the love of Jesus to where it's most desperately needed and hardest to find.

I will never forget stopping for a bite to eat at a fast

food restaurant in Silverdale, Washington. We had five children at the time and had to wait patiently as we made our way through the roped-off maze in order to get to the counter to place our order. We happened to be in line behind an older man who was pushing a woman in a wheelchair. She had trouble deciding what to get, but eventually settled for the salad bar.

Everyone in the restaurant including my family couldn't refrain from looking at the salad bar area when the woman in the wheelchair started having a nervous fit. Her companion tried to pacify the woman the best he could. He gently asked, "Dear, would you care for some carrots on your salad?"

> The woman in the wheelchair started having a nervous fit.

"Carrots! What?" You could tell she was deeply distressed by the mere mention of the vegetable. "Yes. No! I mean, I don't know!" she said with disgust. "I can't believe I'm here without my nerve pills! How come you brought me here without my nerve pills? What about my medication?" she clamored. "Give me celery. No, give me carrots. I mean, no onions. I don't want that! Why'd you give me that? What am I going to do?"

My family watched as the poor man was publicly humiliated. Finally, he wheeled her to a table and went to get his salad. All five girls agreed when one of them pointed out, "Daddy, that lady needs Jesus."

"And she's fixin' to get Him, girls," I assured them.

As the man went for his salad, I thought I'd take advantage of the moment. "Ma'am, I couldn't help noticing something. You're having a real hard time today, aren't you? I'm a Christian, and in fact, I'm a minister. I wonder, would it be okay if I prayed with you? Jesus is the answer to your problems, ma'am. Could I pray for you?"

I was waiting for a cane to come flying out from behind the wheelchair. The devil told me, *This will be historic. You're going to get arrested for badgering an old lady in a wheelchair! There's goes your ministry!* When I realized the devil didn't want me to do it, I figured God did.

"That would be nice. I'm a Christian, too," she said slowly.

"I wanted you to know something," I shared openly. "I know what it's like to feel as if any moment you could lose your mind and never get it back. I also want you to know that Jesus healed my mind. He restored me completely, and since then I've experienced more peace in this world than I ever imagined existed."

Tears were streaming down her cheeks. Everyone watched as I prayed for the distraught woman. I held her hand and offered a nice, general "Chill out!" prayer.

"What are you doing?" her husband said, rushing to her side. His lower jaw had bottomed out with alarm when he saw me with her.

"Thank you, Reverend. I feel so much better. Be quiet, dear. He prayed for me. I'm going to be okay."

Her husband's anguish started to lighten. "I've never seen her so exasperated, and now she's peaceful," he admitted. "Without her medication!"

"None of our ministers ever prayed like that for me," she confided. "You know, I don't get out often, and I never get to be with children," she said softly as she eyed the Nissl-ettes, my affectionate term for the Nissley girls. "We had one son but he died when he was only five. I couldn't have more, so I don't have grandchildren. So, you see, I don't get to hug any children. Nowadays you have to be so careful about touching children. Innocent people can get accused of doing bad things to children." She looked saddened by that fact.

> The girls each took turns hugging and loving on the lady who needed Jesus.

"Well, we have plenty of kids!" I said quickly. "You can hug on 'em all you want!" As if on cue, the girls came running over to their table. Leah tried her two-year-old best to climb up to get a hug. The image of little toddler sneakers jammed in the spokes of the woman's wheelchair will be engraved in my mind forever. Rachel, Bethany, Melody, Deborah, and Leah each took turns hugging and loving on the lady who needed Jesus.

CHAPTER FOUR

Stealing Satan's Children

Evil exists and has a plan but God always has a better one. That's the message of this chapter. The events chronicled here occurred over a two-year period and revolved around an outreach Christ In Action organized in Key West, Florida in 1987. About a hundred Christians joined Denny and other street ministers at a church in Key West for the purpose of going out on the streets to talk to people about Jesus while participating in a Halloween Festival.

The intensity of what takes place in this chapter may shock people. Some of what is recorded throughout these pages reads like a horror novel. It seems unbelievable. Do not be deceived into doubting the authenticity of these events. Denny continually contends with evil. I would say his commitment to ministry has made him one of satan's worst nightmares.

Strange things happened as I prepared to take Sandy and the children to Key West, Florida, for the 1987 Fantasy Festival Halloween Outreach. For the first time in the ministry's history, things did not work out for Sandy and the children (three of them at that time, and a fourth on the way) to come along. Plans flew apart and unusual events dictated that my family would have to stay behind. I knew God had called me to a ten-day, water-only fast, and while I didn't exactly know why, I was sure God meant business. It took two years to unravel the mystery behind God's strict requirement and to understand fully the reason circumstances were what they were that particular year.

Years before this particular Fantasy Festival outreach, a battered old hearse captured my attention and instantly became part of our vision for ministry. To me, it was crystal clear: God wanted Christ In Action to own and restore the dreary funeral car, a 1971 Cadillac hearse. God gave me those instructions and again I didn't have the complete explanation. I only knew that God would bless the ministry as I continued to obey His peculiar requests. Twenty-six coats of shiny black lacquer were not enough to satisfy my friend, Ed Campbell, whom God brought into our lives that same year. It would take one more coat to bring the hearse to the point where Ed felt it would be good enough for Christ In Action. God knew I didn't have the skills to transform the old car into a spit-shined parade vehicle and witnessing machine for Christ. But Ed

Campbell did, and that hearse saw many seasons of use in God's ministry.

Complete Obedience

Some people live to celebrate Halloween, especially in the city of Key West, Florida. Fantasy Festival was the city's attempt to describe a fun-filled time of make-believe for all who might come; however, some that came to frolic in the darkness found a life-changing Light instead in 1987.

> Christ In Action showed up with the shiny black funeral car.

In keeping with the mood of the celebration, Christ In Action showed up with the shiny black funeral car, a sepulcher on wheels, and about a hundred soul winners from all over America. It was destined to be a rare event, as we suspected right from the beginning.

The entire team went through an unusually intense time of prayer and spiritual warfare, which was the first definite clue that something profound was about to unfold. During the morning time of prayer, several Christians indicated they felt exceptionally strongly that God wanted His people to go to certain areas of the city at certain times, to stay away from particular areas altogether, and to be off the streets by a specified time. Because these Christians sensed urgency within God's message, they were willing to be completely obedient.

And, as a result, the most unexpected and amazing turn of events took place. These unusual episodes weren't caught on film by the media but were etched in the hearts and minds of people and most importantly, in the Lamb's Book of Life.

Our fear-inspiring hearse was entered as a float—an entirely appropriate display for Fantasy Festival's Halloween parade. It was well received until we arrived at the judges' stand. The crowd didn't like the DON'T BE CAUGHT DEAD WITHOUT JESUS sign that was plastered over the back window of the hearse. ETERNITY WILL BE HELL WITHOUT JESUS appeared on both side windows. Christ In Action's messages for the day were not welcomed.

Six pallbearers wearing tuxedos and dark glasses walked behind the hearse while I drove. The Christ In Action team looked like a pack of spooky Blues Brothers, which was great because they captured the crowd's attention. Naturally, there was a casket inside the hearse. The metal body box was not, however, filled with a corpse but with a very alive street preacher.

"Look everyone! They're stopping!" the parade announcer pointed out. "There's something very—well, here's something to see folks. What is that? It appears, ladies and gentlemen, there's a casket coming out of the hearse. Wait! It looks like they're going to open it! Why would they do that? What could . . . ? Oh, look! There's someone . . . " the announcer's tone suddenly changed, "Uh, there's someone preaching!" She made no attempt to hide her feelings. You could tell she was disgusted.

With a powerful, handheld, public address system known as a half-mile hailer, the resurrected corpse started his horrifying presentation. "Standing in front of the judges' stand reminds me that one day we will stand before God Almighty, the judge of all judges. He's the one we should fear! To fear God is the beginning of wisdom. Are you wise enough to acknowledge the one who can judge whether or not your heart is in right standing with Him? Will you . . . "

> Each parade entry was allowed a three-minute presentation.

I had done my homework and checked with the parade officials. They informed me that all parade entries were permitted to do a two to three-minute routine or presentation while in front of the judges, so I told my preacher to plan on giving the listening audience a three-minute shock treatment. Thirty seconds into the routine a police officer began tapping vigorously on the window. I could feel him screaming at me but I didn't look at him. I was determined to let the full three minutes go by.

"You can't do this! Get this thing out of here! Hey, do you hear me? I said get this thing out of here! If you don't move this thing, I'm going to get a tow truck in here and haul you away! Now move it!"

He ranted and raved while I looked at my watch and

checked the rearview mirror to see if the casket had been returned to the hearse. When it was safely secured, I rolled down the window and said, "Oh, I'm sorry. Did you want me to move?"

By this time the policeman was blistering mad. He looked as if he was going to explode.

"All-righty then, we're outta here. Have a nice day, officer!" With that, I pulled away. For the grand finale, fifty Christians buried in the crowd whipped out signs, placards, and giant foam hands with the pointing index finger—the kind sports fans bring to cheer on their team. Ours were imprinted, "Jesus is #1." The entire group then filed in by rank behind the hearse, and the entourage retreated into the distance.

Judging by the crowd's animosity, I decided that the hearse would have to go into hiding, so we took the long way back to the church where the group was staying and camouflaged it when we got there. But the outreach had only just begun. It was time for the soul winners to go out on the streets and talk to people about Jesus.

Spirited Halloween Harassment

It came as no great shock when the police started to pester the outspoken Christians on the streets. However, the intensity of their harassment seemed exceptional, and in keeping with the true spirit of Halloween. In one instance, a man preached a message of hope and salvation on a street corner while his partner handed out "What's Wrong with Halloween?" testimony tracts to people passing by.

"Hey, I want you to know if that guy doesn't stop what he's doing, you're going to jail," a policeman declared to the young man handing out tracts.

"So, if I rob a bank, you're going to arrest that guy over there?" the soul winner asked politely.

The harassment got so severe I felt it was time to confront the chief of police. When I arrived at police headquarters, I waited longer than most people would because I was determined to question him. I waited patiently until he agreed to see me.

> The harassment got so severe I felt it was time to confront the chief of police.

"Your police officers are harassing us, and I'm not going to put up with it. Could you please tell me which law we've broken?" I asked.

The chief of police would not respond until I gave him the name and phone number of Christ In Action's attorney.

"We've successfully sued another city right here in your state, and we'll sue you as well if you don't get off our backs. I guarantee you, you will hear from my lawyer. I've studied the laws that pertain to what we're doing here, and we're not breaking any. If one of your officers finds that someone from our group *is* breaking the law, I want you to contact me," I said, handing him my business card. "I give you my word, I'll deal with them more severely than you would. Do you understand? Now, I suggest you let us go on doing what we're doing, and you will have saved this city a lot of money."

Midnight, October 31

Three days later, on Halloween night, I took a team of Christians for a time of casual praise and worship on a street that had been blocked off to accommodate pedestrian traffic during Fantasy Festival. It didn't take long for what looked like a majority of the police force to show up with a brigade of paddy wagons. We were surrounded on three of four sides. The team knew I wanted them on their knees. If the righteous were going to be hauled away for praising God in public, then I wanted the righteous to make it difficult.

I held the microphone and started preaching the message I felt God had given me for the citizens of Key West. A crowd had gathered to see what was going on. Naturally, I ended with an altar call. "Folks, a lot of you out there are attracted to the bizarre and occult nature of this pagan holiday called Halloween when what you really should be looking for and celebrating is Jesus, the Lord of lords, the Light of this world. Won't you give your life to Him? He died a bloody death for you. Talk about bizarre! Jesus spooked everyone when he didn't stay dead. . . . "

Afterward, the chief of police came over and said, "Reverend Nissley, are you done?"

"Yeah, I'm done. Can I ask you a question? Why'd you bring all those paddy wagons?" I looked to the chief of police for an explanation.

"When I heard you guys were having a religious rally on Halloween night, I thought there might be problems. I brought the paddy wagons in case anyone gave you a hard time. We were prepared to haul them away. We're here to make sure you have your right to preach the gospel while in Key West, Reverend Nissley."

Devil Worship Exposed

By the next day the city started to return to normal. People left Key West in droves. They put away their spooky costumes and went back to their normal routines. The hordes of visitors returned to their hometowns, including a man from Anchorage, Alaska, his wife, and their twenty-four-year-old, pregnant and unmarried daughter.

It came to my attention much later that the man from Alaska was the third-ranking man in the Satanic Church. The daughter, who was four months pregnant, was carrying her father's baby in her womb. The infant had been conceived with one purpose in mind: to become the next "Most Unholy High Sacrifice" for the Satanic

> The child of incest was to be satan's sacrifice.

Church. This satanic priest had come to Florida to lead a satanic conference over Halloween. Unbeknownst to the Christ In Action team, there were hundreds of satanists in town during Fantasy Fest. They were there with the express purpose of opposing Christian influences. In fact, we found out they had been specifically instructed to haunt soul winners and to intrude on Christian activities.

But a strange thing happened. The devil worshippers could not find a single Christian. They never came in contact with any Christians when they went out on the streets looking for them because the Christians were mysteriously absent. Remember how explicit God had been when He directed the group to be at specific locations at particular times and to avoid certain places at other times?

Then the satanists discharged a team in the middle of the night early in Fantasy Fest to go to the church where we were staying to cast spells on God's people. That was the plan until they came down United Street and attempted to cross the street. There was no perceivable obstruction or visible barrier, but when they tried to go towards the church they were supernaturally restrained and physically unable to cross the street or leave the sidewalk on the other side. They left confused and infuriated. Not willing to give up easily, they tried again the next night. The same thing happened.

As the festivities started breaking up, even the satanists had to get back to their jobs. When the priest found out that the cursing of God's church had not taken place, he became so furious he decided to return to Florida taking his wife and daughter with him. They checked into a motel and went to United Street at midnight, searching for the church where the Christ In Action teams had stayed. He looked forward to invoking his master's avenging powers, but much to his surprise when he stood across the street from the church and attempted to go forward, he couldn't cross the street either!

He tried with all his might to do this simple task but he, too, was mysteriously restrained and physically unable to leave the sidewalk. After several attempts to cross the street, he was fraught with hellish anger and ordered his family back to the motel. Seething and raving like a madman, he scared his own family. His daughter's attempts to encourage him to calm down and cool off were in vain. "Father, you're way too angry! You've got to chill out!" she said as she took off to go for a walk.

Switching Sides

The priest's daughter walked around the outskirts of Key West only to end up back on United Street. There she saw a light in a second-floor apartment window near the church, and for that reason, she crossed the street without a problem.

"Hello?" She introduced herself to the church's

youth pastor and his wife, who happened to live in that apartment and be up at that late hour. They invited her to come inside.

"I've got to tell you something. Please believe me when I tell you this. My father is the most powerful man I've ever known. You must understand something. Whatever, and I mean whatever, my father wants, my father gets!" she said as she cradled her slightly swollen belly. "In my whole life, I've never seen him fail at anything!" She proceeded to tell the story of the invisible wall at the sidewalk across the street and the devil worshippers' frustrated attempts to interfere with the concealed Christians.

"Except this church and that group of Christians, my father has always gotten everything he has ever wanted. I know now that God has more power than satan does. I want to serve God," she concluded.

> "I want to serve God."

The satanic priest's daughter gave her life to the Lord that night in the youth pastor's living room. They had a time of deliverance casting out the demons she had grown up with probably since before birth. They prayed and dedicated the baby in her womb to Jesus, and before the sun came up the next day the woman left Key West to go into hiding under a fictitious name.

Inevitably, the people involved in the Fantasy Festival outreach quickly rose to first position on the devil's

"Top Ten Hit List" after brazenly stealing his Most High Unholy Sacrifice.

One Year Later

The Fantasy Festival outreach was scheduled for October of the following year, however, things were again not normal, and again my family was prevented from coming. Our host church in Key West received a call from someone on staff at Bob Larson's "Answer Man" show. The caller said he wanted to notify the church leaders that Anton LaVey, the founder of the Satanic Church and author of the Satanic Bible, had called in to the show and mentioned that church specifically. He felt LaVey's comments could be construed as a hostile threat, so he decided to forward the information.

The pastor from the church called another minister who was instrumental in helping to organize the outreach, who then called Christ In Action's office to tell me about the devil's attempt to intimidate us. LaVey had mentioned last year's Halloween conference on the Larson show and intimated that his group had experienced some setbacks, but things were looking better for this year's meeting. LaVey had said something to the effect of, "You tell those people. I want them to know, this year I'm not sending a boy to do a man's job."

I came up with a message of my own. I figured if the devil had my picture circulating in his ranks, I would do the same. I made sure every Christian at the outreach saw a mugshot of LaVey's face.

"Hey, gang!" I said, holding up the photo. "This guy's in the crowd and he needs Jesus! Don't be afraid of him. Cast the devil out of him." That was my message to the soul winners. And once again I told them to fast and pray.

Three days into the outreach, two soul winners were passing out tracts and talking with people on the streets when suddenly the girl recognized a familiar face.

"Hey, that was Anton LaVey!" she told her partner. "Hey! Anton! Anton LaVey!" she called out into the crowd. "Yo, Anton, wait up. Anton!" He turned and looked at what he must have known were spirit-filled Christians.

"Devil, I bind you in the name of Jesus! I bind you and your works . . . " the girl shouted. The devil's CEO took off running like a scared jackrabbit. The Christians chased him as far as they could into the crowd but eventually lost sight of him. Later that evening when

> The devil's CEO took off running like a scared jackrabbit.

they gave their report back at the church, the entire team got to hear about the exploits of the two fearless young believers on a mission from God.

I summed it up by saying, "Hey, gang! Guess what! We got the devil's Most High Unholy Sacrifice last year and this year we've got his chief executive officer on the run!"

A battle was won for the Lord because a handful of seriously committed Christians were passionate about winning lost souls for Jesus. They sought God on their knees and laid prostrate on the church floor in intense prayer for hours because they knew the enemy had it in for them and was conspiring to destroy them. They fervently called out to God with all their strength, crying tears of compassion because of their desire to see people won to the Lord. And it paid off, big time!

Clearly, people heard from God as He literally directed each and every step of the outreaches. The devil had his goods stolen, "Halloween-ers" came to Christ on the most diabolical anti-Christian holiday of the year, and soul winners witnessed the indisputable, pitiful, impotent condition of the enemy as the devil's true nature was unmercifully exposed. It was no wonder my family couldn't come to Fantasy Festivals. I know why God directed me to a water-only fast for ten days. We couldn't have accomplished much for God if we had not made ourselves available to God's power and anointing. When we needed it the most, His power was there. God showed up and showed Himself strong on our behalf, and He received all the glory.

More Unnatural Events

I was emotionally, physically, and spiritually drained after that exhausting week, yet on the way home I had two flat tires in Miami and had to have the hearse towed. After the repairs were completed, I was geared up to see my loving family and nobody else. Although I was thoroughly worn out, I was eager to get back home to Chicago, so I decided to drive all night.

I was traveling outside of Nashville on Interstate 24 when I noticed a bubble in yet another tire. I didn't believe it was natural to have so many tires go bad, but not having a choice in the matter, I had to deal with it. At 7:30 in the morning the rush hour traffic was surging and vehicles were swarming all around me. When the opportunity presented itself, I pulled over on the shoulder just before an exit ramp and tried to inch my way to the exit. That's when the police car came out of nowhere.

"May I see your license and registration, please?" the officer asked.

"Sure thing," I replied. "Is there a problem, officer? I'm trying to get to a service station before I blow another tire. I just replaced two tires down south." I wearily pulled out the receipts from Miami to prove my level of frustration was unfeigned.

"I see," the officer said. "Would you mind pulling up and parking in the grassy area over there?"

"No, sure thing, officer," I said. "I hope this won't take long. It's been a very long week. I just want to go home."

It took longer than I expected. When I saw several sets of flashing lights on what I assumed were emergency vehicles, I thought the delay was justified. There must have been a bad accident somewhere nearby.

To my amazement, the emergency vehicles turned out to be the Tennessee SWAT team. Twelve special agents in full riot gear got out of their vehicles and surrounded the hearse, holding their guns with both hands, their weapons pointing straight up in the air. It looked as if they were standing at attention eagerly waiting for their commander to simply give the signal. I remembered the half-circle of paddy wagons in Key West. The scene felt vaguely familiar, but this incident seemed a bit more curious.

> Twelve special agents in full riot gear got out of their vehicles and surrounded the hearse.

"We'd like permission to search your vehicle," the person in charge said.

"For what?" I asked.

"We have strong reason to believe you might be running drugs and or guns."

"Naw, I don't think so," I said. I knew all about vehicle searches and the damage it leaves behind. I remembered what it was like when the police stripped my truck in Pennsylvania back when I really was a drug dealer. "I got a wife and kids I gotta get home to."

"Sir, you should know we will get a search warrant. It will be here in about two or three hours."

"Oh, I see." I thought for a moment. "Well, then, you can search my hearse on one condition. You have to promise to put everything back the way you found it.

And, just for your information, so you're not surprised, there's a casket in the back."

"Oh?"

"Yeah, but don't worry. There's no body in it. It's full of Jesus junk."

"Really?"

"Yeah, really."

They pulled the casket out and unpacked my boxes of Christ In Action tee shirts. Every individual shirt was examined, each collar and seam checked for drugs, every foam "Jesus is #1" hand investigated. After searching and probing through every inch of every possible space, someone said, "Well, Sarg, I believe he's telling the truth. This vehicle is filled with a bunch of Jesus stuff."

Apparently, the route I was taking from Miami to Chicago was renowned for drug and gun running. The officer who called it in felt the time of day and the haste with which I was traveling (as indicated by the receipts I had shown him), indicated the hearse had to be filled with something illegal.

"Listen, can I ask you one favor?" I looked at the seargent. "Can I get my camera out and take some pictures? My wife is never going to believe me when I tell her about this."

Busted for transporting Jesus junk, what a legacy! But that's the type of thing that happens when you're a missionary to America.

CHAPTER FIVE

Into the Neighborhoods

"You can't teach what you don't know, and you can't lead where you won't go." *The contemporary Christian musician Carmen coined that phrase, and the Nissleys live by it. It has taken them into many interesting "neighborhoods."*

Neighborhood is a term used rather loosely here. Some of the episodes in this chapter take place in the Cabrini Green projects in downtown Chicago. And a neighborhood is not what you could call what was left in south central Los Angeles after the Rodney King verdict riots, but that's where Denny and his family ended up staying for over a month to help a church minister to the community. Denny has discovered that the most effective approach to reaching spiritually wayward people is to focus on their situation, go into their neighborhoods, and tell them the truth.

"What are you doing in our 'hood, man? It's after dark," the gang banger declared. "You can't be in here, man. The White man don't live long if he stays here after the sun goes down."

"I appreciate the warning, but I'm already in!" I said.

A bunch of his fellow hoodlums started mouthing off. "What are you, man? You the KKK?"

I looked around to find out who made that ridiculous statement. "Who said KKK?"

"I did," someone confessed.

"I bet you do drugs, don't you?" I said.

"So what if I do?"

"You'd better be on drugs right now to think that I'm that stupid. I might be White, but I ain't stupid. What am I gonna do, come into Cabrini Green with two White guys late at night and yell *nigger?* You're on drugs, pal. I'm a preacher of the real gospel and if I can't bring Jesus into your neighborhood, then your neighborhood ain't worth livin' in. Are you listening to me?"

"You a real preacher?" someone asked.

"Yeah, I'm the real thing."

"Will you pray for my mama? She's real sick, she's bad."

"Yeah, preacher, me too. If you could just pray for my mama," someone else asked. Apparently, kids in gangs have sick mamas and believe in the power of prayer; at least these kids did and that was good enough for us.

At the time, my buddies and I were helping a friend of ours, Dan Taylor, forge the way to begin a new Christian outreach in Chicago's infamous Cabrini Green, one of America's most dangerous housing projects. At that moment, thirty members of the Disciples street gang heard the requests for prayer and flocked together to check out what our response would be. They knew we'd have to go into the high-rise apartment building where elevators were commonly used for death chambers as gang members clubbed people to death. If gang members took us into a dark hallway, there was a chance we might not see daylight again. Nonetheless, we sensed a secret appreciation towards us for intruding on their turf. We brought with us the possibility of repair for their abandoned hopes and forsaken faith.

> Apparently kids in gangs have sick mamas and believe in the power of prayer.

"Okay, let's go meet mama." I swallowed hard.

By the grace of God, the guy with the sick mama lived on the first floor. "You stay outside; I'll bring her to the window," the worried son said. I was relieved.

An anxiety-ridden mother came to the window looking hopeful. She leaned forward onto the windowsill so we could talk about Jesus. Mama was a believer. It was plain to see faith in God had sheltered her from the string of tumultuous storms that constantly raged all around her.

"I'm sick, preacher, because my son's in that gang."

"That's okay, ma'am. We're here to help him, too." I tried to be as comforting as I possibly could under the circumstances. I joined hands with her and prayed to God for strength and healing for her mind, soul, and body. Then she joined us as we all prayed passionately for the community's recovery.

Immediately after our collective amens and shouts of praise to the Lord, someone else asked, "Hey, man, will you pray for my grandma? Could you ask God to take away her pain? It ain't right, her suffering and all."

And the prayer requests came pouring in. We criss-crossed through the middle of the projects in the middle of the night, ministering to the people, and we lived to tell about it.

'Hood Ministry

Before we left I told the gang about Dan. "My friend Dan is coming back here to your 'hood. I want you all to welcome him as you did us. He is coming here because he wants to start a Bible study for your 'wannabes.' I'm talking about your little brothers and sisters. You don't want them growing up to be like you, do you?"

The teenagers looked at each other and then hid their eyes from our view. They were unable to look at us. They knew too well they weren't worthy of a blessing, but desperately wanted it to happen for their families. The desire of their hearts was to see something good happen for their loved ones. Too many of these kids expected to die violently. They were resigned to such a fate because in their minds that was the inescapable destiny life had to offer. To die young was recklessly justified.

> The desire of their hearts was to see something good happen for their loved ones.

It made me sick. It made me weep. It made me want to fight even harder to save souls in Cabrini Green.

"Yeah, Denny. You tell him to come on in. We'll take care of him."

"Good. I expect there won't be any shootin' going on when he's starting up his Bible study. God is God. You treat Him with respect, even in this neighborhood," I told them outright.

"Dat's right. We're cool with God, man."

"That's good to hear. I know if someone killed your buddy, or some stray bullet got your little sister, a lot of you would take justice into your own hands. But we're here to tell you justice has already been taken care of. No one else has to take any more bullets for anyone because Jesus died for all of us. He died for us so we could live free. I admire your loyalty to one another, I really do, but there's something you haven't considered. There's only one Brother who will stick closer to you than anyone in your gang. His name is

Jesus and His power is all the fire power you'll ever need."

That's how we helped start Dan's 'hood ministry, by meeting the needs of the hoodlums. Another Christian ministry was successfully launched in one of America's worst neighborhoods, and as far as I know, no one from God's gang ever got shot.

Whose Turf Is It, Really?

Even Hawaii has some pretty tough gangs. I was blessed to have an opportunity to spend six months ministering in Hawaii, and while I was preaching on a street corner in Waikiki, a big Hispanic boy yelled, "Hey, shut up!"

I saw him and a few of his gang members swarming towards me. "No, I won't. What's up? Are you from a branch of the Boy Scouts? Girl Scouts, maybe?"

"What did you say? What you don't know, mister, is that I can make one phone call and there will be fifty Bloods here ready, willing, and able to beat you to a pulp!"

"Excuse me, did you say one phone call?" I questioned the menacing gang member.

"Yeah, one."

"Would you? Could you? I'd love to have fifty guys to preach to! Can I give you a quarter? You know how a crowd draws a crowd. Would you go call them as quickly as you can so I can have a crowd to preach to? Please, get them down here! Will ya?"

He drew back his arm to lay a monstrous punch on my face but I caught his fist in the air. I remember thinking, *Look what I snagged! Betcha he's not going to like this.* It was a miracle that made me look powerful, so I took advantage of the moment and started squeezing his fingers.

"Now that I have your attention, let me explain how things really are. You're on my turf. It's my territory because the earth is the Lord's and the fullness thereof and you're on a street corner with me, so you'd better be nice and polite. If you can't do that, then perhaps you should leave the island as well. Do you understand this?"

"Yes sir," he said. He backed off and after that day the Bloods would occasionally hang out a certain distance from my street corner, listening to my messages on the sly. One day my family and I walked by their favorite street corner, and the Bloods recognized me. At the time we had five daughters, including Leah, our newborn. "You that street preacher? Those kids all yours, man? They all your kids?"

"They're all mine," I replied. Naturally, I asked them to explain why they called themselves the Bloods, and when it was my turn I talked about blood also. I talked about the power in Jesus' blood that covers the sins of the whole world. They listened while I explained the concept

> I asked them to explain why they called themselves the Bloods.

of a blood sacrifice. It was something they could relate to, and for many of them it seemed to make sense. The gang bangers were ignorant about the blood of Jesus, so I told them, which is what I think Christ would have done if He had been made friends with the Bloods on their street corner. That's what God has called us to do.

Being Dramatic

As well as being an evangelist, I am also a member of the steering committee of the National Street Ministries Conference. The committee decided it would be good to hook up with Phoenix First Assembly for a major outreach. Pastor Tommy Barnett's church at the time could seat 6,500 people. Our goal was to put on an event that would fill the church with troubled youth from all over the area. Billboards were purchased, radio ads went on the air nonstop, and we distributed 38,000 full-color posters with pictures taken from the drama called *Straight from the 'Hood*. A tremendous amount of money was spent to publicize this event. Sometimes, extraordinary things have to be done in order to get ordinary people saved, but it's always worth every penny.

Pastor Barnett sent twenty of his buses out and retrieved over a thousand kids from the streets. The other 5,500 must have gotten there on their own because the church was filled to capacity. Bags were searched for drugs and checked for weapons with metal detectors. Staff members put up with a lot of rude behavior but approximately 1,500 kids came up front to receive Jesus as their Savior at the altar that night. Almost a quarter of the audience came forward for prayer! Drug addicts, prostitutes, runaway kids, and members from rival gangs stood together at the foot of the cross asking for God's forgiveness.

Sonny Argunzoni preached the altar call. "I believe the Bible is true and the Author who wrote it lives in my heart. This book tells me that you can be forgiven, no matter what you've done, no matter what kind of life you've had! I know because I've been where you are, and I thank God that I was smart enough to believe Him at His word! Let's ask God to heal our hearts. Let's let God in tonight."

> God came in and cleansed away the guilt and shame of hundreds of teenagers.

I watched reverently as God came in and gently cleansed away the guilt and shame of hundreds of teenagers.

Ground Zero

But there are more troubled neighborhoods than there are street preachers. Sometimes Christ In Action acts as a stimulus to get churches or other ministries going or serves as the support system in crisis situations. This was the case in 1996 when my family and I traveled to south central Los Angeles to help a church called Victory Outreach.

I parked my nice bus on a nice concrete slab that may once have been a nice building. The building had burned down in the riots after the Rodney King verdicts were announced. Although it had been years since the riots, it was pretty obvious we had parked in a war zone. Racial tension was in the air, so Victory Outreach posted a security guard outside the bus twenty-four hours a day so no one could damage it or try to steal it. Even though the community was making an attempt to reduce crime, the citizens hadn't entirely given up their appetite for violence.

Victory Outreach wanted to offer the community healing through an impressive one-day street party and festival following a week of outreach. They blocked off three blocks and seven lanes of traffic at Manchester and Broadway, the exact epicenter of the riots. They set up a stage with a backdrop and a powerful sound system with tower speakers. Musicians drew crowds in with Christian rap, rock, and reggae. They had a low-rider bicycle and car show, plenty of good food, and a steady stream of people all day. Then, at dusk, the Victory Outreach actors and actresses filtered themselves out of the crowd and into position for the performance of the drama.

"Listen, officer, we want to let you in on a secret," a Victory Outreach leader told the policeman in charge. "We're getting ready to put on a drama that's seriously realistic. It's called *Straight from the 'Hood* but the guns and blood are not real. It's all Hollywood. We're going to scare some folks tonight, but we don't want it to be you."

"Good idea. I'm sure glad you told us."

"We're hoping to scare people right outta hell and into heaven," I informed him.

"May I suggest you double-check your props? We wouldn't want any accidents to happen out here tonight." Victory Outreach gratefully accepted the advice and double-checked everything for the play.

About a thousand people gave their lives to the Lord that night at the altar call after the forty-minute drama. Christians then ministered to victims of violent crimes one-on-one. The pastor had an altar call for crime victims, and six to eight hundred people flooded the front area. Then he made another announcement and something remarkable happened.

"If anyone has bigotry in their heart, pray and let God heal you. Let Him forgive you and then go find a member of another race and give him or her a hug," the pastor said to the crowd. "Say something like 'I forgive you' and hug their neck till God says let go. Would you do that tonight? Let God have His way tonight, people. Don't be stubborn. God's not pleased with the rebellion that's taken place here, but He stands ready to restore you and this community because He is the God of love and restoration. Let's get rid of the hate. Shall we?"

People started to openly hug people. It was not what the police and the community expected would take place at our post-riot rally. I had a line a half a block long because I was the only White man in the area at the time. I thought, *Am I ever going to see the end of this line? And Lord, they're all waiting in line because until today they used to have a problem with hatred—towards me! What if someone's not completely healed?* I stood out in the crowd. In fact, during the weeks my family and I had been in Los Angeles, we were the only White people we saw for days at a time.

As I embraced one person after another, I felt the presence of God dissolving an assortment of hard-heartedness, and I started to cry. One Black man hugged me and turned to walk away, but I grabbed him by his jacket and said, "You didn't give it up, did you? You still hate me, don't you? You don't like the White man, do ya? I know where you're at because I used to be a bigot. I used to hate Black people. I used to hate people just because they were Black. If you'd just release it to God and give it up, God will set you free to love all people. Trust me, it's true."

> I felt the presence of God dissolving an assortment of hardheartedness.

He looked at me for a good while and when the wall of hate fell, we held each other and wept, right there in south central LA, right there where years before people had killed people just because of the color of their skin.

I found my wife later and asked her, "Sandy, did you see what happened when the pastor dealt with hatred between the races?"

"I sure did!"

"Did people form a line to hug on you and the kids? They did with me. For over an hour, I was a White hugging post!"

The police said they had never had that many people in one place at one time before. They wouldn't have allowed it; the potential for trouble was unthinkable. But God showed up in the 'hood and there was not one arrest, distress call, or major problem.

A Reason to Preach?

My self-appointed title is "missionary to America," but I think I need to change it to "missionary to America and beyond." I never know who will be affected by my preaching or how far God will take me into the kingdom of darkness to be a beacon of His glorious light, but since I've been willing to preach for little or no reason, the results have been blessed. In this case, all it took was an ugly necktie.

My ugly necktie is black with the names of famous streets all over it in bright colors—Rodeo Drive, Wall Street, Park Avenue, Bourbon Street, and so on. My friend Rick Hagans thought that as a street preacher I should have a street necktie. I think the devil invented the necktie, but what he meant for bad God can use for good.

At one point in my ministry career, I realized I had preached on nearly all of the streets on my tie except for Abbey Road in London, and thus I developed a desire to preach on Abbey Road. I eventually ended up in

London, found Abbey Road, and discovered the famous street is in a residential neighborhood. The street is lined with row homes except for Abbey Road Studios made famous by the Beatles and one high-rise apartment building. There I was, so there I preached.

I looked around at all the people not there. There was no one to preach to except a few squirrels playing around. Just so I could say I did it, I decided to preach anyway and asked myself, *What exactly do you preach*

> There was no one to preach to except a few squirrels.

when no one's listening? I used my imagination and envisioned hundreds of people and lifted my voice for about twenty minutes proclaiming the plan of salvation while my friends Martin and Daryn walked around looking for someone to hand a tract to. I thought, *This is brutal! What a waste of time! Not a soul in sight! The squirrels must think I'm the one nut they'll never crack.* And then, a few minutes into the experiment, I felt a special anointing of God, and I knew God wanted me there. I told myself, *Someone must be listening or I wouldn't feel this.* When the anointing lifted, I stopped and looked around. Things did not look promising, but Martin was talking with one exceptionally animated guy across the street.

"Brother Denny! Come here!" Martin shouted. "Meet the Sheik."

"Hi, I'm Denny Nissley."

"You are fundamentalist, no?" Not waiting for my reply, he continued, "I said to myself I must go meet this radical fundamentalist who preaches when there's no one to listen, yet I hear his words through my closed windows. I am fundamentalist Muslim. I am pleased to meet my brother."

"Ah, Sheik, I'm glad you came out and all, but I am not your brother. To be brothers, you and I would have to have the same Dad. God is my Father and yours is the devil."

"God is my father, too!" he protested and then spat on the ground in disgust.

"Not the God of the Bible," I insisted.

"God of the Quran!"

"See, what did I tell you? Different."

The sheik started to shake. "You Americans! I dislike you Americans."

"That's all right," I told him. "If I weren't a Christian I wouldn't like you either."

He spat again. For about an hour we discussed religions and world events. I found out that this man was one of the most influential Muslims of our time. Ironically, he was raised by Catholic nuns in Mexico City, educated in the United States, and received his Ph.D. in Berkeley, California, yet he hated Americans.

"What do you think of Louis Farrakhan?" I asked.

He spat. "Louis Farrakhan is not a fundamentalist!"

"Hey, I agree with you, but don't spit! What do you think about Libya's Muammar Ghadafy?"

"He is not a true fundamentalist," he said after spitting one more time for emphasis. He went on to explain fundamentalism in general and Islamic faith in particular. The conversation was intriguing. I'll never forget what he told me that Muslims believe about souls. According to this man, Muslims believe that a thief probably won't change; therefore, when a Muslim kills a thief he is stealing the thief's soul from the devil and the soul goes to heaven. But if a thief happened to die in a car accident, Muslims believe the

> If a Muslim kills a thief he does the thief a favor.

thief's soul will go to hell. When Muslims kill people they truly believe they're working for God. Only the Truthgiver could set them free from that murderous lie. As I listened, I waited for an opening in the conversation.

"Muslims can't marry a woman unless her father is a keeper of the book," the sheik informed us.

"What book?" I asked.

"The Quran, the Bible, or the Torah, any of those three."

"So, you read the Bible? Who is Jesus to you?"

"Jesus was a prophet, a good prophet."

"Well, I have to tell you Jesus said, 'I am the Way, the Truth and the Life. No one comes to the Father except through me.' And if Jesus is the prophet you say He is, then that pretty much cuts out Allah, and Mohammed is toast."

"I don't like you Americans! If you speak against the

Quran, we will kill you. You will die! I know you speak out of ignorance, or I should kill you here and now!"

"Well, I'd have to say you don't know me very well because I speak against it quite often!"

He was furious, yet curious about what or who made me so bold. We talked at length about what he thought should be done in Jerusalem. I, of course, told him what the Bible says about Jerusalem. Despite our differences, he liked me well enough to invite me to attend his family's mosque in Lebanon if I ever found myself looking for a famous street corner in his country.

"I have never heard Christianity explained this way in all my life," he admitted before we parted company.

I was amazed. This ardent man was raised by nuns and educated in the United States, but it was because of an ugly tie that he stopped long enough to talk to a street preacher about Jesus and examine Christianity from a new perspective.

CHAPTER SIX

Taking the Cross to the Million Man March

It is hard for a street preacher like Denny to resist a crowd. Denny's stature and his voice command people's attention and make him stand out in a group. Give him a ten-foot wooden cross and put him in a rally with a million Black men, and you could be sure he would get their attention. Nonetheless, Denny knew God wanted him to proclaim the gospel message at the Million Man March in Washington, D.C., in October of 1996.

Denny was not deterred by the message he received that preaching at the rally might be life-threatening for him, a White, Christian street preacher. He therefore wasn't entirely surprised when an angry mob searched for a rope to hang him from his own cross. But God had a different plan in mind.

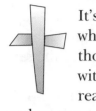It's always a temptation for me to preach when a large crowd is gathered. This time, though, I was not so sure. Looking back, it's within the realm of divine possibility that the real reason a million Black men came together was to hear the gospel preached. But as I cut firewood on the Saturday morning before the Million Man March, I wrestled with a desire to preach there. *Do you want me to go, Lord? I want to be sure that you want me there,* I prayed.

I received my answer: "Go to the Million Man March and preach, but I want you to know the enemy has an assignment for your life."

I turned off the spinning chain of the saw. "Am I going to die?" I asked out loud. Silence. "Am I going to live?" Nothing. All I knew was that God wanted me to go to the rally, and the enemy was going to try to take my life when I got there. Now my problem became how to inform Sandy. *Hi, Honey. It's Saturday. I might be dying Monday.* I told her I was going but kept my concerns in my heart and continued to pray.

Sunday Morning

During the announcements at our Sunday morning service at Manassas Assembly of God Church, my pastor, Charles Nestor, declared to the thousand or more churchgoers, "Denny Nissley's going to the Million Man March tomorrow. Let's remember to keep him in our prayers." There was some concern on his part—apparently my going to the Million Man March was a big deal to Pastor Nestor. And, immediately after the service, a distinct trend began to take shape.

I will always obey the prompting of the Holy Spirit to go somewhere to proclaim the Good News, but it's highly irregular for the Holy Spirit to tell other people that I might die doing it. A woman found me in the lobby and said, "God told me to pray for you while you're at the March." She paused. "Brother Denny, God told me to pray for your life." I locked eyes with her somewhat surprised.

"Then girlfriend, I suggest you pray," I said.

From the foyer, a brother backed me into a corner to say, "About that rally, I'll be praying for you. God told me to pray for your life, Reverend Nissley."

"I really hope you're obedient, brother." Hmmm.

> I decided to get my affairs in order before Monday morning.

When the same thing happened in the parking lot, I concluded people were onto something. These independent confirmations validated my word from God. I continued to pray and also decided I would need to find time to get my affairs in order before Monday morning.

Sunday Afternoon

Someone from the church's outreach ministries team

had obtained a permit for that Sunday afternoon to preach on the steps of the capitol building, the precise location of Farrakhan's impending address. A few church members and I took a handheld public address system so we could proclaim holy ground and make a stand for truth at that historic site. There were hundreds of Black men hanging around waiting for the main event to begin in less than twenty-four hours.

After singing a round of praise and worship songs, the Christians began preaching over the public address system. We came face-to-face with an entourage of Nation of Islam men whose demeanor seemed to suggest "Touch me, and you will die!"

"Hey, how come you're protesting?" one man spoke out.

"I ain't protesting nothing. I'm proclaiming." I said nonchalantly. "There's a big difference."

"What are you proclaiming?" asked an authoritative-looking man in a bow tie.

"Salvation through Jesus Christ and Him alone," I answered. "I'm proclaiming liberty in Christ." A conversation about doctrine followed, and I shared the plan of salvation with him. After a brief time, the group of Nation of Islam members left.

Since the gospel can't be preached openly in Islamic societies, many Muslims have never heard the Good News, met a true Christian, or seen a Bible. Some face certain death if they convert to Christianity. Nevertheless, I couldn't stay away when the outspoken leader of the Nation of Islam, Louis Farrakhan, opened a spiritual umbrella under the guise of a sacred assembly, touting "atonement for all" in hopes of persuading more Black people to commit to the cause.

The wind of truth began to blow through Farrakhan's assembly when some soul winners showed up with their weatherworn Bibles, a small public address system, and a crazy street preacher with a ten-foot cross.

A Divine Appointment

"Do you know who that was?" someone in our group asked after the authoritative-looking man left.

"Yeah, a Muslim," I replied.

"Yeah, a Muslim by the name of Dr. Abdul Alim Muhammad."

"Oh," I said, unimpressed. "Dr. who?"

"Abdul Alim Muhammad—Minister Alim. He's Louis Farrakhan's right hand man for this march, and one of the highest ranking men in the Nation of Islam. Everything goes by him."

"Still a sinner," I said.

The Christians returned to their assignment of worshiping the Lord. Forty-five minutes later, a motorcade of Nation of Islam vehicles stopped in front of the team, and Minister Alim confidently approached.

I could hardly contain my delight. "Hey, you're back! I know, you want to repent and become a Christian, right?"

"No."

"Why are you wasting my time then?" I asked in an overly sweet tone.

Minister Alim let out a muffled laugh and admitted, "I like you."

I immediately asked him to write his name and phone number on a 3" x 5" index card and then handed my business card to him. "This is your lucky day. I'm gonna let you buy me lunch sometime," I said. And then I added, "I eat a lot."

"I like you," he said again.

"You said that twice," I informed him.

"I like that cross," said Minister Alim.

"It's all right. The original one was better."

"I would like this cross to be in my March tomorrow."

"Well, it's my cross."

"I would like you to carry it."

I was dumbfounded. "You want a White man to carry the cross of Christ in a Black Muslim rally?"

"Yes, it's a Day of Atonement. Everyone's welcome—White man, Jew, Asian, Indian, Hispanic. Everyone's welcome. It's the Day of Atonement."

> "It's the Day of Atonement."

"That's great! Little did you know, I'm going to be in your March tomorrow," I informed Abdul. "Look for me. I won't be hard to find. White guy with a cross, that'll be me."

"You wait for my phone call," Abdul said. "I'm going to call you." But he never did.

Sunday Evening

Our group returned to Manassas later that night to attend the Sunday evening service. Pastor Nestor once again announced his desire to pray for me. Out of the blue, he asked me to come forward so the elders and the staff could lay hands on me and pray for the Million Man March outreach.

I thought, *This is getting intense. He's never called me up front before.* The prayer focused on my physical safety and included a plea to spare my life. There it was again! Something was definitely brewing.

Before leaving the church, a Black brother told me he wanted to go along to the March. I thought it would be good to have a Black man with me at a Black man's rally. I invited him to come home with me that night to sleep on our couch so we could get an early start. I planned to leave at 4:30 in the morning in order to find a decent place to park.

As Sandy and I got ready for bed, I decided it was time to confront my wife with the seriousness of the situation. "You know it can get pretty, ah, intense tomorrow."

She turned around from where she was standing and stared at me. "I know. You know you could die tomorrow," she said matter-of-factly.

I thought about that for a moment and said, "Yeah well, I could die any day on the freeway. Why'd you say that?"

"I didn't want to tell you, but, ah, I was praying and the Lord told me you were going to go and He also told me you might die."

"Wow! Guess what God told me while I was cutting wood on Saturday? Why didn't you tell me?"

"I didn't want to worry you. Why didn't you tell me?" she asked, already knowing the answer. My wife, the mother of our seven daughters, expecting our eighth child, received the same answer.

"I didn't want you to worry." I told Sandy I was willing to go to the Million Man March if that's what the Lord wanted. We both had faith to believe that God was able to deliver, that was never the question. The fact was God's plan might not include deliverance, and it had to be said out loud.

> God's plan might not include deliverance from harm.

"God is able to deliver, but there's a chance He might not. So, there's no problem. I'm going?" She nodded. "Since we don't have a problem with my going, there are some things I'd like to tell you."

We stayed up until after two o'clock in the morning getting our affairs in order.

"I have a will prepared," I told my wife. "Call the board members. They'll all come. God will supply for you and the girls." The tedious task ended with the discussion of our life insurance plan. When we felt we had covered all of the details, Sandy asked, "Do we wake up the girls?"

"No, I don't want to worry them."

The hardest part was telling my wife what to tell the girls. "Tell them I'm not afraid of dying. Tell Rachel . . . Tell Bethany . . . Tell Melody . . . Tell Deborah . . . Tell Elizabeth . . . Tell Leah . . . Tell Grace . . ." The emotional exhaustion of it all came crashing in. I took a quick shower and fell into bed.

Two hours later, I got ready to leave, stepped outside my bedroom and saw my second oldest daughter, Bethany. "Hi, Dad!"

I thought, *Bethany, do you always hang out here at 4:30 in the morning?*

"Just wanted to say good-bye one more time, Dad."

I tried to hold back the tears. "Bye, sweetheart." I hugged my daughter for what I hoped would not be the last time. I found out later that Bethany, who was eleven at the time, went into her bedroom and prayed from 4:30 to 5:30 that morning.

Monday Morning

The outreach team had gone to DC on Sunday, when they had a permit, but there were just two of us going for the actual march. When my lone companion and I arrived at Union Station with the ten-foot cross, we were immediately barraged with media. "Who are you? Why are you here?" they asked us. I answered the question by starting to preach, saying, "I'm here to share Christ."

Someone yelled out, "Hey! This isn't a religion thing. It's a Black thing!"

I looked out at some angry faces and shouted as loud as I could, "No. That's where you're wrong! This isn't a skin thing. It's a sin thing!" It became the theme song for the day.

> "It's not a skin thing. It's a sin thing."

My friend and I continued walking towards the Capitol. "You are the craziest man in the universe!" my companion exclaimed.

I quickly assessed my helper. He was a hard-core, beat 'em up, shoot 'em up, former gang banger from the West Coast. Both parents had been killed in drive-by shootings, and he had been in and out of jail since he was fifteen years old. He was a real tough guy, but even he wasn't comfortable in our situation. Unless I called him over to where I was standing, he stayed a safe distance from me. I never felt more alone with Jesus in all my life.

We walked on and set up our cross alongside the Capitol building. When I started preaching, it was 8:00 A.M. March attendees gathered around. Some seemed enraged by my preaching and proclaimed their intentions. "Let's hang him. That's what they did to our forefathers!" a couple of leader-types yelled. Several other obedient men started combing the area for a rope. "Yeah, let's hang him from his own cross!"

Meanwhile back at the Nissley home, at 7:30 in the morning Bethany woke up her older sister, Rachel. "What are you doing?" Rachel asked her sister.

"We need to pray for Daddy!" Bethany insisted. The two oldest Nissley girls prayed from 7:30 to 8:30 the morning of the march. My life depended on God and the prayers of godly children and obedient saints.

As the mob got more riled up, I considered the likelihood that Daniel might have had the opportunity to guess which lion would be the first to grab him for lunch. *Which angry man will throw the first punch? Will my wife and children see my name in tomorrow's headlines? I wonder if I'll make front-page news? Could this be the event that sends this street preacher home to be with Jesus?*

I asked God, *What do you want me to say? What can I say that won't arouse their wrath?* Someone in the crowd wanted to know what color Jesus was. Another person was concerned about specific doctrinal issues.

A voice cried out, "Was it Ishmael on Abraham's altar? Yes, I believe it was Ishmael on that altar!"

"Wow," I exclaimed. I was amazed, but not dazed. Quiet inspiration came to my rescue. "You must be a theologian. I'm just a dumb street preacher. You know what? You might be right, but answer this question, who was the ram in the thicket? Who was the sacrifice that God gave in place of Abraham's son? You see, I'm here today to tell you, a million of you, that it was Jesus who was sacrificed! Today, it should be your behind and mine on the altar, but we can't pay enough to cover our sins. The substitutionary ram was Jesus, and He died for the Blacks, and the Whites, and the Asians, and the Hispanics. He

> "Who was the sacrifice that God gave in place of Abraham's son?"

died for us all! Let's say Ishmael was on that altar if you like it better that way. That's fine with me, but answer this question, will you bow down to Jesus? Will you put Jesus where He belongs? Will you . . . "

That was not the sermon they came to hear. A guy in a crisp bow tie came face-to-face, nose-to-nose with me and proceeded to shout, "Shut up! Shut up or I'm going to knock your head off!"

"What's your name?" I asked.

"My name's Brian," he said spitting. "I don't hang out with White trash."

"Okay, Brian. I'm going to let you in on a secret."

The disturbance was growing and drawing attention when two police officers suddenly came out of nowhere. "Is there a problem here gentlemen?" They looked at the two of us, trying to size up the situation.

"No, sir, no problem here. Brian and I were just talking." Immediately after the officers left, I made sure Brian knew I was there at the Million Man March as the invited guest of Dr. Abdul Alim Muhammad. I showed him the index card with Minister Alim's name and phone number. "Remember, it's the Day of Atonement, Brian. Everyone's welcome. And, for your information, Minister Alim and I are going to have lunch together. You see, Brian, Minister Alim is interested in my cross. And there's something else you should know. Evidently, he's not consumed with hate and vengeance, and he's certainly not interested in hanging me from my own cross." Brian finally left in a huff and melted back into the crowd.

Out from the Crowd

The crowd's intensity, however, did not diminish when Brian left. But about ten minutes later I saw a sight that made me stop and stare. In all my life, I had never seen a more beautiful sign. The white, hand-painted sign with blood red letters read: JESUS SAVES—ONLY HE DELIVERS.

I saw a Black arm holding the sign but he was an ocean away. Keeping my eyes fixed upon the sign, I realized it wouldn't be long before the sign carrier would see my ten-foot cross in the sea of humanity. Eventually our eyes met and after several prolonged moments we found each other within the thickening crowd.

"I love you, brother!" the man shouted as he let his sign drop to the ground. We hugged one another joyfully, both of us thrilled to find an ally amidst the crowd. Since I wasn't expecting any support, when I saw a fellow Christian come out from the multitude, I figured I was looking at an angel.

This Angel Can Preach!

That angel, Warren, took on the adversary fearlessly, fully engaged in the battle for men's souls. "Who can deliver you Black man? Muhammad? Allah? They cannot! Bring me the man who can deliver you! Is he Farrakhan? I tell you the truth, Farrakhan cannot deliver you." Warren began fervently preaching some radical material. He paused only to look at me long enough to ask, "Am I doing all right? I've never done street preaching before."

"All right?!" Grateful for this unexpected help and astonished by this brother's boldness on his first day on the job, I quickly added, "Brother, you keep it up! You're not bad for a rookie!"

But venom, hate, and murder oozed from the eyes around us. Why did all the angry guys seem to show up at our location? When the crowd's collective pent-up aggression looked as though it was aimed for a deadly assault on Warren, I started preaching to shift their animosity to another target. The minute the attack got too heavy for me, Warren started back up again.

Like a tag team, the two preachers kept going for over an hour, until a determined "committee" decided to put an end to it. The Muslims extended a personal challenge to their brother, Warren.

"Brother," their leader said, "why don't you join your Black family? We've put on the biggest family reunion ever. The whole family's here. Why don't you leave this ugly piece of White-trash, fat garbage and join your family?"

> Like a tag team, the two preachers kept going for over an hour.

Warren looked at me, then at the crowd. He looked at them individually while they anxiously waited for his response, and then Warren locked eyes with the leader of the pack. "Family," he shouted, "is not about the color of your skin!" He had their attention. "You don't get it, do you? Family means you have the same Father. This piece of White trash and I have the same Father. Our Father has an only Son, who happens to be heir to everything the Father has, and we've been adopted into the Father's family. Only thing is, because of our sins, the Son had to die in order for us to get in. We're brothers because of the sacrifice of the Father's Son! The Son's name is Jesus, and the Father raised Jesus from the dead—took Him right out of the grave, overcoming death and defeating hell itself. The Father promised we would do the same if we would accept His Son, Jesus, whom He sent because He loves us."

Warren took a deep breath and added, "And by the way, this means Jesus whooped Allah a long time ago!"

They didn't like hearing that. I immediately thought, *Dude, you're gonna get us killed. But hey, at least I'm going to heaven with an angel!* It had occurred to me I might die that day, but I never thought I'd be departing with an angel named Warren.

Warren concluded his passionate speech. "Listen to me. It's our Father who will one day say to Louis Farrakhan, 'Go to hell. I don't know you.' This is what will happen to your leader if he doesn't repent before God for his sins."

Feeling restored, I added, "Will our Father look at you and tell you, 'Go to hell' because He doesn't know you either? The Bible says we must be born again. I don't know for sure the color of Jesus' skin. I don't know and I don't care. But I do know the color of his blood. It was red."

Warren and I preached side-by-side until we both felt that we had accomplished what God had sent us there to do. We embraced again, said good-bye, and went our separate ways. The young man from my church and I headed back to the van.

Monday Evening

I couldn't wait to rejoin my family. We met at a sand-wich shop where I was overcome with emotion when I saw them all. I hugged my wife and children, drinking in their love. It was as if I was absorbing everything I possibly could from them.

"Daddy! Daddy's home!"

"Dad," Rachel unburdened herself. "I am so glad to see you! I prayed for you, Dad. And when I was praying for you, God had me pray for your life! I just felt as if the devil would try to take your life! Tell us, Dad. What happened?"

"Rachel," I said with tears in my eyes. "Thank you for praying! If I had a dollar for every time someone threatened my life, I could pay off our mortgage! If I had another dollar for every time someone asked me what color Jesus was, we could eat really well for at least a year!" I told my wife and children what happened.

I told them that each time I tried to inject the salvation message into the Million Man March, someone in the crowd went into a frenzy. But I lived to tell about it. The enemy never likes it when I invade his turf, but God doesn't mind. In fact, he sent me an angel named Warren to prove it.

CHAPTER SEVEN

Making Mardi Gras into Mardi Grace

New Orleans during Mardi Gras is hostile territory for church folk. The Mardi Gras season officially begins on January 6, the Feast of Epiphany, which honors the day the three kings visited the Christ child. Mardi Gras officially ends with Fat Tuesday, the day before Ash Wednesday, which is the beginning of Lent. Revelers come to New Orleans from all over the world to make sure that they have something to repent for during Lent. It's the ultimate "Party-Now-Pay-Later" plan. The Mardi Gras celebration sanctions sin and promotes promiscuity the like of which has not been seen since the days of Sodom and Gomorrah.

This chapter is a medley of Mardi Gras experiences covering a number of years. Since 1979, Denny has challenged people to reach out beyond what's comfortable and to grow in their walk with the Lord by going to Mardi Gras. It is one of those extreme growth opportunities. It can have a life-changing effect on both Christians and non-Christians. I know. I've been there.

The kind of ministry that takes place during Mardi Gras has a flavor all its own. Anywhere else, it would be completely outrageous. In New Orleans at Mardi Gras, it fits right in.

One year a pastor from South Carolina decided to experience New Orleans for himself. He came up with an unusual method of getting people to listen.

"I have to have your attention," the pastor-turned-street-preacher announced. "Yes, you! Everyone up on that balcony. I need you to listen to what I'm getting ready to say. Give me your attention. Please, I must have your attention," he declared matter-of-factly. "I'm going to UNZIP . . . my coat . . . ALL THE WAY!" Without exception, every head on the balcony turned to see whatever it was he was going to expose, their flesh so addicted to sin that they couldn't help themselves. The befuddled crowd watched as Pastor Mike exposed his shirt, and then they heard the unzipping of a rookie street preacher's mouth: "God loves you! No matter who you are, no matter what you've done! You don't need to drown your sorrows with alcohol! Jesus can fill you with Living Water so you'll never thirst again."

That's how the gospel is preached on Bourbon Street, and that's what I love to do—unleash men and women of God on the streets to preach the Good News. Since I can't preach salvation to all of America myself, I set my face like a flint to set ablaze people's passion for winning lost souls for Christ. The streets of New Orleans are swarming with needy people. The soul winner wonders, *Which one, Lord? Which poor soul do you want to reach through me?* That's why I have strict requirements for those who come to a Christ In Action outreach.

Soul winners must be ready to do spiritual warfare, which includes prayer and fasting before the event. Once on site they're required to follow the schedule and rules explicitly. If they don't, they're sent home at their own expense. Each day begins with mandatory quiet time—Bible reading and prayer—followed by an hour or more of praise and worship and a time of exhortation and teaching. It's vitally important that the troops prepare themselves spiritually before they go out to battle.

> It's vitally important that the troops prepare themselves spiritually before they go out to battle.

The devil doesn't like it when Christians go directly into his territory to retrieve souls. I won't ever send anyone out onto the streets thinking they're fueled up on their own strength. Christians who want to discern and experience divine appointments must first acquire a divine anointing by denying their flesh, emptying themselves, and filling up with God. If they're willing to do that, I know they will do some serious damage out there on what used to be the devil's turf.

Vagabond Rebel Teens

While there seems an inexhaustible supply of needy

people on the streets of New Orleans, none are more ominous than the gutter punks, whose world is especially dark. New Orleans, a haven for this "tribe" and their beloved dogs, can support five hundred or so gutter punks, but there are probably thousands migrating all over the country. New Orleans has what they need—abandoned buildings, dumpsters, a Bohemian party atmosphere and, during Mardi Gras, plenty of half-full cups of beer and booze to be picked up off the curb or scarfed from trash cans and table tops.

In the middle of Mardi Gras in 1996, the people of New Orleans made it their mission to run the gutter punks out of town. When I heard that, I knew it was time once again for Christ In Action to take the love of Jesus to where it's most desperately needed and hardest to find—to the social outcasts recognized for their lawlessness and grunge.

> The people of New Orleans made it their mission to run the gutter punks out of town.

The punks were being arrested for crimes such as "impersonating a human being" and petty things like "blocking a public walkway" because they scared the tourists. The New Orleans merchants, fed up with their panhandling, public urination, drunkenness, and fighting, circulated posters picturing the gutter punks and stating: DON'T FEED THE ANIMALS.

To me, the gutter punks looked like a cross between the hobos of the '20s and '30s and the hippies of the

'60s. Although some people thought they acted like animals without souls, God showed me they were made in His image and it was for them Christ died. They had no defenders—that is, until some spirited Christians showed up with a message from Calvary.

People on the streets have the same basic desire as everyone else to belong to a loving family. The gutter punk kids are convinced they've found the family they need in each other.

The year 1996 became the year of ministry to the gutter punks as Christ In Action teams encountered the transient teens throughout Mardi Gras. One team showed a genuine sensitivity towards them.

"They don't like being called gutter punks," Jerry told his partner, Linda.

"Yes they do," Linda said. "They'll tell you that's who they are. I gave a balloon sculpture to these three earlier and they seemed genuinely touched." The scruffy-looking girls wore mismatched clothes probably rescued from a Salvation Army store. One girl looked as if she was dressed in a deteriorating quilt. Pieces of outdated garments, most of the fabric soiled or frayed, had been sewn together randomly and appeared to be someone's attempt to create a long, warm, winter garment.

"Bet you thought we would hurt you," one girl blurted out.

"No," Linda said. "Why would I think that? I don't know anything about you. Who are you?"

"I'm Sky. This is Eyelet, and this is Patches. I thought maybe you heard about us from the TV. They said we beat up tourists and stuff like that."

"My name is Linda, and this is Jerry. All I know is that you live on the streets because you choose to. You're making a statement or something, I suppose."

"A statement? You think I'm here by choice? If I had a place, I'd be in it right now watching *Ricki Lake* or *The People's Court* with Judge what's-his-face."

"Oh, I see, I guess. Well, would it be fair to say that aside from your housing arrangements, you're living what you believe? Kinda like what Jerry and I are doing?"

"Living what you believe," Eyelet repeated the phrase thoughtfully. "Yeah, that's cool."

Linda shared her testimony with Sky, Patches, and Eyelet. The girls, drawn in by Linda's story, spent twenty minutes absorbed in the highlights of Linda's ravaged and redeemed life. Jerry had quietly planted himself in the background and prayed God would save their souls and keep them safe from harm. Linda listened when they opened up and shared their beliefs. Never once did she whip out her Bible and point her finger in condemnation, although she quite effectively spoke the Truth in love. It ended with a group hug. Both team members understood that the Holy Spirit would have to convince, convict, and comfort the young women. "Listen, you girls take care of yourselves." Linda found it hard to let them go. "It's a very dangerous world out there."

I had instructed the soul winners to "love on" the kids first. Linda had listened. She concentrated on connecting with the kids to establish a relationship with them so that maybe someday it would pay off. Obviously, gutter punks have some crazy, messed-up values, but to a discerning heart willing to look closer it becomes apparent that these kids align themselves with people who care. They value relationships.

"We're feeding the tribe tonight at the 'wall.' Tell all your friends," Linda added. "Tell 'em we'll have vegetarian stew and plenty of dog biscuits!" The wall refers to the end of Elysian Fields Avenue at Decatur Street where a wall separates the French Quarter from the Mississippi River.

"Wow, that's so cool! People don't do stuff like that for us. We'll be there!" The girls sauntered off into the crowd.

Extreme Evangelism

Actually, we brought much more than dog biscuits. We had 80 gallons of hot chocolate, 700 cans of soda, mega-coolers full of hot vegetarian stew, 1,000 hamburgers, and some packaged condiments. "The wall" became an outdoor restaurant for the homeless. We also had a van full of clothing, 300 wool blankets, and hundreds of pairs of new cotton tube socks to give away.

> "The wall" became an outdoor restaurant for the homeless.

"Hey, preacher!" someone yelled out. "Someone told us you brought dog biscuits. We want to feed our dogs before we eat."

"That's too bad," I answered using the microphone. "We're feeding you first!"

"Then we won't eat!" the rebel replied.

"That's fine with me. Jesus died for people, not dogs. You're more important to Jesus than the dogs are. Because you don't know God, your priorities are out of whack. But hey, if you insist, my crew will pack up the food and . . . "

"Wait! Uh, no, don't do that, man. You promise to feed the dogs?"

"Yes, as soon as we're done feeding you! Listen up, I came here from Washington, DC. These people helping me came from all over the United States of America. We heard the police were trying to run you out of town, and we want you to realize we came here because we give a rip about your lives. The police don't love you. They don't even like you. They want you gone!" Since I knew they hated most Christians, I said using my best preaching voice, "And, oh, by the way, we're Christians. We want to feed you because we love you. We want to be a part of your family tonight. I know some of you think we hate you, but you're wrong. We love you. Look around. There are hundreds of Christians here lovin' on you! We took time off from our jobs without pay to be here. We left family behind to be here because we heard about your plight. We were concerned when we heard about your situation on TV. Now, let's thank God for the grub."

After my speech, they were respectful and even polite. I'm sure people were surprised when many of them bowed their heads for prayer. Then, one by one, they cheerfully came through the food line. And they showed how much they cared about each other.

"No thanks, man, I already had some. I don't need it, but my friend does. Can I have this for my friend over there?" one boy said pointing to a slumped-over kid.

The punks sat in groups of six or eight with one or two of us. The Christians had sweet fellowship with the angry White rebels called gutter punks and a few homeless people. Amazingly, after a short while, the bone through the nose didn't matter. The peacock colored hair and the hateful tattoos became pretty much invisible. The outreach was such a success I decided to do it again on Monday night and announced my intentions over the microphone with instructions on how to get a free blanket and some socks.

Monday night it rained, so we covered ourselves with plastic trash bags and fed them again. I overheard one kid telling a soul winner, "Hey, remember me from the other night? You said if I found you here tonight, you'd give me a blanket."

"We ran out of blankets but I saved one for you behind the seat of my truck. Wait here; I'll go get it."

"Thanks, man," the kid said. "I really blanking appreciate this. Now I can sleep." He paused. "Ya know, ain't nobody ever stood out in the rain with us—ever!"

We hadn't planned on such a strange outreach but God must have because we were reaching people from all walks of life. My mother, along with most of the Christ In Action kitchen crew, came Monday night to witness firsthand the unusual ministry. Through an open window in the back of our van, my mother overheard a conversation she'll never forget.

"Do you know what kind of Christians these are?" a guy asked his friend. "They're religious, but ya know what I think? I think this is what Christians should be doing."

"I don't know, man. I can't figure it out, but I agree," his friend answered. "And they're not shouting at us either!"

> "I think this is what Christians should be doing."

We did give them the message, though.

Testimony Time

There's nothing more exciting for an evangelist than to lead someone to the Lord. I love to reel them into the kingdom of God, especially when I pull them out of the devil's sea of despair. I'm overjoyed when I get to be a part of someone's salvation experience, but the greatest part of my ministry experience comes during testimony time when I get to hear ordinary Christians tell their extraordinary stories of God's love and grace. Some soul winners can't get a good night's rest until they've shared their victory stories, so each night I let them do it no matter how late it is, no matter how exhausted we are. Not everyone hits a home run every time at bat, so testimony time also provides much needed encouragement for those who may have struck out on the streets.

Back at the church just outside of New Orleans it was two o'clock in the morning when Martin couldn't wait to share. "I felt like the Lord was telling me to just talk. I believe He was showing me that because of my peculiar accent people would listen to me and what I had to say. So, that's what I did, Brother Denny. I chatted all night long and now my voice is completely gone, glory to God!" reported Martin, a banker by trade, a soul winner by grace.

"I want you all to know," I spoke out after the laughter subsided, "Martin's from London. He's here on holiday! That's British for vacation, y'all! Martin, are you having a good holiday?" I asked in my best British accent.

"You know I aa-amm, my braa-tha!" Martin answered in his best southern drawl.

"Anyone else?" Denny asked the ragged group. A young man stood up.

"Brothers and sisters, I don't know if you noticed it or not, but there are a lot of backslidden Christians out there. One of them urinated on the cross when we were preaching on Bourbon Street, but as soon as he zipped up his pants, the power of God hit him so hard he fell to the ground sobbing like a baby. So I grabbed Brian and Dave and went over to him. We knelt down beside him, put our arms around him, and prayed with him, right there in the middle of the street! It was at the foot of our peed-on wooden cross that the backslidden Sunday school teacher rededicated his life to the Lord!"

The saints celebrated God's mercy with renewed fervor, even though prior to testimony time any measure of physical strength we might have had left was nearly extinguished from laboring on the streets all day and night.

"But that's not all! Brother Denny, when we got up from our knees and took him off to the side, he was completely sober! He knew exactly what he was doin'! We took him to a pay phone so he could call a cab. He wanted nothin' to do with Mardi Gras! Isn't God good, y'all?"

The happy hollering went on until I told the exhausted group, "Get out of here, you bunch of fanatics! You Jesus lovers! Ten minutes til lights out. Good night!"

"Vait! Brother Denny! You must tell dem about us!" someone called out in a heavy Russian accent.

"Oh yeah! Folks, wait just a moment. You won't believe this! We happen to have with us two Russian evangelists from Pennsylvania. It was their turn to go to the microphone and read the Bible." (Each year at Mardi

Gras teams from Christ In Action read through the Bible in its entirety in Jackson Square. We set up a booth next to the soothsayers and fortunetellers to read God's Word aloud and to pass out free New Testaments to people.)

"I asked them to read in their native language and guess who just happened to be in the crowd at the time? Two Russian businessmen! When they heard their native tongue being spoken over our puny sound system, they rushed over to see what was going on. They had never heard the Word of God before! They prayed the sinner's prayer with our Russian evangelists and received Christ as their Savior! God's Word is powerful in every language, Amen?"

> Two Russian businessmen prayed the sinner's prayer at Mardi Gras in New Orleans.

Each year when I think, *God, it doesn't get any better than this*, more amazing stories come pouring in off the street, some from the most unlikely places.

A Child Shall Lead Them

The Nissley children have been to Mardi Gras every year and as they grow older, they, too, have come back with tremendous stories. In 1998, my twelve-year-old daughter, Melody, found herself involved in a story she felt might end up, in fact, in the pages of this book. As she told me about her encounter with a fortuneteller, I agreed. This adventure was worth recording.

"Come with me. You've got to meet her!" Melody said.

"Meet who?" Jodie asked Melody.

"The fake astrologer! You've got to meet her, I told her all about you!"

"Wait a minute, darling," Jodie said with concern. "First of all, what are you doing hanging out with astrologers, and second, what did you tell her about me?"

"I told her about the book you're writing. Come on, let's go. It's not what you think, just come on." Melody grabbed Jodie's hand and dragged her away from the wall where she was seated in historic Jackson Square in New Orlean's French Quarter. I was glad Jodie went along to find out what Melody had gotten herself into.

Even though it was Mardi Gras, I never expected Christ to show up in the person of a fortuneteller with a faux leopard scarf. Gretchen Martin had her audience targeted. Her card table resembled the other dozen or more soothsayers' and fortunetellers' tables alluring the unsuspecting as they walked by. A pile of colorful, over-sized, laminated cards covered the center of a painted tablecloth. Arrows pointing every direction flowed out from what appeared to be an exciting focal point.

When Gretchen was between customers Jodie introduced herself. "Hi, I'm Jodie, the writer Melody was telling you about. You must know I was worried when Melody said she was friendly with an astrologer." Her looks were her hook. She was every bit as enchanting as the real thing. "Would you tell me about your ministry here?" Jodie inquired.

Gretchen told Jodie how she counsels customers about their future but instead of giving them a bunch of devilish hocus-pocus, she enlightens them with the Truth. "I see only two lines," she says, making a cross in the unsuspecting client's palm. "They both come to an end as will your life, and if you like I'll tell you why these two lines cross and how it may affect your future." Gretchen gently holds the hand with both of hers and looks compellingly into the client's eyes.

"Do you know what these two lines mean? God is letting you know His Son Jesus died on a cross like this. Did you know that He did it because He loves you? Jesus does love you. The Bible tells us God doesn't want us to turn to, or seek out mediums or fortunetellers. The Bible warns us that they will defile us. The Lord wants you to know He is the Lord, your God, and He loves you, enough to die for your sins."

Without letting go of the hand, she then turns each brightly colored card over one at a time. A super-condensed picture story version of God's plan of redemption unfolds. "See here? Jesus was born of a virgin. God sent His Son to earth as a baby to be like one of us. He grew up and taught God's truth in the temple, but the religious crowd didn't accept Him. See here?" She turns over another card. "He performed miracles and healed people. Jesus is the real hope of the world. He is the hope you're looking for and your future is in His hands."

She thoughtfully reveals all the cards beautifully depicting the gospel message until at last the centerpiece is unveiled: There is ONE GOD. With the client's hand resting gently in her palm, she asks him or her to pray with her. At the session's conclusion, the fake astrologer gives each client a handout containing Scripture verses to confirm her statements.

God had given this woman a very unique ministry. She knew God would hold her responsible for what took place at her card table and for that reason, she made sure praying Christians constantly surrounded her. She came to Mardi Gras from Oklahoma. Camped out in the devil's playground where lies are sold for five bucks a pop, Gretchen made sure God's truth, the Truth that sets people free, was not only available but tangible.

> She knew God would hold her responsible for what took place at her card table.

I asked my daughter, "How'd you know she was a fake?"

"Well, you see Dad, I asked her if she would read my palm."

"You what?" I was shocked.

"Here, take a look!" She unfurled the inside of her palm showing me a message written in ink: JESUS LOVES YOU. "I went to Jackson Square and asked all the fortunetellers to read my palm!"

Of course she did. She's my daughter.

Small, But Mighty

Melody's sister Deborah was a preteen in New Orleans in 1999 when she handed a gospel tract to a homeless man on a bench.

"Give it to someone else," he said. "I can't read."

"I'll read it to you. It's my dad's testimony. It's a great story. It's called The Funnel."

He sat up straight. "Yeah, I guess that'd be okay."

"My name's Deborah Nissley. What's yours?"

"Johnny," he said with a smile. He looked pleased someone had paid him some attention. Johnny had managed to get by living on and off the streets most of his life. After spending fifteen minutes with my daughter, Johnny was nearly weeping.

"Thank you little Debbie," he said. "Ya know, you're the first person ever to talk to me about Jesus." The forty-four-year-old man was sincere. "Could you explain it to me?" he asked Deborah.

"Sure, Johnny. My dad, you see, was a really bad man. He got into drugs and stuff he shouldn't have. The devil messed up his life, but God put it all back together. He got saved when he asked Jesus to forgive him of all his sins. He had a really bad accident and the doctors were going to cut his leg off, but God healed him and now he's a preacher."

"Little Debbie, do you think I could get saved like the man in the story?"

"Yes, sir. Would you like me to pray with you? All you have to do is ask Jesus to forgive you and He'll come live inside your heart." Johnny repeated the sinner's prayer with eleven-year-old Deborah.

I arranged to meet Johnny the next day. Johnny told me his greatest desire was to get off the streets. He said he was willing to do whatever it took, so we brought him back to the church for a shave, a haircut, and a bath. Afterward, Johnny hopped in our family van with seven other homeless men to go to His Place, a ministry home in Alabama for men like Johnny, founded by Rick Hagans and his wife, Kim. Johnny's parting words were, "Denny, I wanna learn how to read. I wanna learn about Jesus. Give that little Debbie a hug for me! God bless you! God bless you all!"

I'm sure that someday Johnny will read, hopefully before he leaves His Place. By virtue of God's grace and the goodness of our little girl, I know what Johnny will choose to read.

People who go to Mardi Gras in hopes of experiencing the ultimate street party should be told there's no comparison to the feasting that will take place at the banquet table of the Lamb! Somebody has to tell them that what they're really looking for takes place in heaven. And they ought to find out what they must do in order to be there. Thankfully, each year Johnny and hundreds of others like him receive the Word and are able to find Christ . . . in action on the streets of New Orleans during Mardi Gras.

CHAPTER EIGHT

This Is America, Right?

"Repent! Turn from your sins!" That's what some people expect from a street preacher, and it might arouse hostility or at the least some spirited resistance in an irreligious crowd. On the other hand, experiencing the same results to "Hark the Herald Angels Sing" should be cause for concern, especially when sung together with a crowd of Americans waiting for a Christmas parade to begin. Unfortunately, this was the situation when Denny was arrested for demonstrating without a permit in December of 1998. The charges were dropped, but because of Denny's willingness to fight for his first amendment rights, the town of Manassas, Virginia, had to re-examine its laws.

Denny is adamant about the fact that when people stand up on public property to proclaim Jesus, or satan, it's illegal for anyone in America to stop them. Preachers of the gospel shouldn't fear the competition, only the prevention of free speech. Denny's messages to Christian audiences usually include a reminder that believers should regularly exercise their freedom to proclaim the Good News.

The first time I got arrested for preaching the gospel in a public place was during our first year in the ministry in Greeley, Colorado. Christ In Action took in a grand total of $6,500 in 1982, so when I called home to tell Sandy I needed five hundred of those dollars to make bail, I might as well have asked for fifty thousand.

"Honey," Sandy had it all figured out. "Why don't you just sing? They'll let you out!"

I knew back then that it was my privilege as an American and my responsibility as a Christian to fight for my right to free speech. I was more than willing to make it an issue and inclined to make a federal case out of it. Consequently, I did end up in federal court some years later.

Jailbird for Jesus

During spring break of 1985, I worked with a youth group from a church in Lakeworth, Florida, on the streets of Fort Lauderdale. A group of us were walking down the side of the street, which was packed with bars, restaurants, and gift shops. Sandy was out in the crowd taking pictures, and I was carrying the cross.

I found two college students standing in line waiting to go in one of the trendy bars on the strip. It was around nine o'clock at night and the two students seemed interested in talking with me, so I took the cross off my shoulder, propped it upright, and stood in line with them while we talked about Jesus.

Out of nowhere came a deep voice, "Hey, buddy, you've got to keep moving. You're not allowed to stay still, that's loitering."

"Oh, really?" I asked the police officer. "Why can't I wait in line like the rest of the people?"

"Because I said you can't. Now move it on down the street," he said pointing.

"Okay, I'll go," I said as I picked up the cross. "But I don't understand why it's okay for these people to loiter."

He screamed as loud as he could, "Because I told you to move it!" He was a substantial 6'4", 240 pound law enforcer with an attitude, so I decided it would be best for me to leave. I hadn't taken three steps when another police officer stepped right in front of me.

"Take it beachside!" he snapped.

"What?" I asked.

"Take it beachside!" he repeated pointing to the other side of the street. As he pointed, he swung his fist six or seven times, throwing upper cut punches to my stomach, knocking me off balance, and pushing me off the sidewalk. I tried to keep my composure, so with the cross still on my shoulder, I assured him I was going.

> As he pointed, he swung his fist six or seven times, throwing upper cut punches to my stomach.

"Why are you hitting me?

I'm leaving! I'm going!" I turned to walk across the street when all of a sudden the officer started flipping out. He yelled to the crowd, "Stop him! He's under arrest! You're under arrest!"

The crowd started yelling and the scene quickly got chaotic. Someone jumped me from behind and the cross fell to the ground. Someone had a professional chokehold on me and with his forearms locked around my throat was trying to expose my neck by pushing under my chin. Luckily, I caught a glimpse out of the corner of my eye and saw it was the other police officer trying to strangle me.

I kept my chin down, put my hands up, and said, "Okay, man. Take it easy. I'm leaving!"

Suddenly he thrust his knee into my lower back to elongate my spine so I would raise my chin. His arm came in directly under my adam's apple, and I went out like a light.

I awoke on the hood of a police squad car. While I was unconscious, they had ripped my arms behind my back so hard my shoulder ligaments tore out of their tracks in the shoulder joint. My larynx and trachea had been crushed, splitting open my voice box. As they put me into the police car, I turned, glimpsed Sandy and saw the flash of her camera. They shoved me towards the open door but miscalculated their aim and smacked my head into the side of the car, and then someone said, "Oh, yeah, I forgot. Watch your head, Reverend."

I was taken to a holding station and left there for two and a half hours. At the time my physical condition was pretty bad. My shoulder throbbed, the muscles in my back twitched in torturous spasms, my hands cramped up due to the lack of circulation, and when I asked if I could use the bathroom, they had a good time laughing at me. They told me I'd have to wet my pants. I was somewhat relieved when I heard, "Nissley, let's go. You're moving on to Central Lock-up." My only prayer was that there would be a bathroom at Central Lock-up. Thank God there was!

A One Word Bible Study

Nearly two hours went by before they took the handcuffs off. My hands and arms fell to my side limp and aching as the blood rushed back into them. My fellow jail mates were drunks and street people except for one fellow who let it be known he was a millionaire businessman with a foul mouth who was in for drunk and disorderly conduct.

"Well, Reverend, whatcha in for?" he asked.

"I'm here for preaching Jesus to two college students in front of a bar."

He wandered off only to return after a short while to ask, "Well, Reverend, what's the word for today?"

"The word for today is the same for everyday. The Bible says the wages of sin is death, but the free gift of God is eternal life in Christ Jesus." He slapped me so hard across my face it stunned me. I quickly prayed, "Jesus, don't let me hurt this man!"

He walked away and returned to ask, "What's the word *now*, Reverend?" I shared with him the next part of the gospel story, chapter and verse. He slapped me again, leaving my face stinging. After about half an hour, he returned and we did an instant replay, but this time when he walked away I grabbed him by the collar of his expensive suit.

> He slapped me again, leaving my face stinging.

"Tell ya what, mister. You seem to be interested in words, so we're going to do a little word study here tonight. The word *grace* comes to mind. You've experienced this three times already this evening. Let me explain it to you. Grace means having unmerited favor given to you even though you don't deserve it. God's grace allowed me to restrain myself three times tonight, but I'm deeply concerned you've reached your limit. You see, God's grace is far more sufficient than mine. If you hit me again and I retaliate, I want you to know that God did not fail. I failed God. To make it simple, the next time you hit me, I might flush you down that toilet and if that happens, don't blame God, blame me."

He rolled his eyes.

"Do you understand this?" I asked.

"Yes, Reverend. I do." He didn't bother me again with his vain attempts to dishonor God. In fact, he was rather courteous during our remaining time together. It was three o'clock in the morning when they finally let me out on bail.

Do Right, It Pays

Due to my injuries, my medical bills were substantial so I contacted an attorney. He suggested we sue the city of Fort Lauderdale, the police officers personally, and the bar due to the fact that one officer was a paid employee of the bar at the time. It took four and a half years to go through the system, but justice prevailed as I told my attorney it would. I attached myself to Romans chapter 13:3 that says, "For rulers hold no terror for those who do right, but for those who do wrong. Do you want to be free from fear of the one in authority? Then do what is right and he will commend you." I had faith to believe that I would be commended.

Sandy and I agreed to let God be in control throughout the entire ordeal, and He rewarded us by letting us see His hand at work in every aspect of the incident. Before the case was over and a verdict announced, all kinds of people acknowledged God's sovereignty, especially those who had witnessed the trial's eight days of scrutiny. Because ours was a first amendment and freedom of religion case, we received media attention and extensive press coverage. Law students were assigned to the courtroom to study the arguments. It was major news—the city of Fort Lauderdale, police officers, and a bar getting sued by a street preacher for seven different violations of the law!

Getting God into the Courtroom

Before the trial began, the attorneys on both sides grilled the potential jurors on their spiritual beliefs. I took detailed notes. Our jury ended up with two Jewish women, a couple of lukewarm Christians, one backslidden fellow, one man under the influence of a born-again fiancée, one undecided, and so on. The temptation to preach was overwhelming. I informed my attorney that sometime during the course of the trial I wanted the opportunity. He thought I was being too radical, but having looked at my notes from jury selection, I knew precisely what these individuals needed to hear. How could I not preach?

Of course, my opportunity was provided for me when I was asked to demonstrate for the court exactly what it was that I did on the streets. I said, "I'd be happy to, but it might get a little loud, Your Honor."

"That's all right, Reverend Nissley. Just give us a sample of what you do," my attorney prompted.

"Okay, then, I might say something like, ladies and gentlemen! There are people within the sound of my voice who may not know Yeshua is Jesus,

> "That's all right, Reverend Nissley. Just give us a sample of what you do."

the Messiah, the One sent from God. There are some that know all about Jesus, the Messiah, because you used to serve Him but you've gone astray. There are others who say they know Jesus but it's all in their heads. The Bible calls such people lukewarm and says God will spit them out of His mouth. Some may not have decided whether they even believe there is a God." I mentioned every single juror's life situation and then closed with the salvation message using a judge's perspective. "God is the just judge who judges all men's hearts. He's holy and . . ."

It quickly became apparent the evidence in the case weighed heavily in our favor. Sandy had not only taken photos of the beating and false arrest, but a pastor from Fort Lauderdale just happened to be in front of the bar with his video camera and got the whole thing on tape! When the defense tried to discredit the amateur videographer/pastor as a witness, it came out that this man was not only a pillar in the community but he had also served as Fort Lauderdale's police chaplain. His testimony revealed that the Fort Lauderdale police department hired him to provide videography instruction, which became a real problem as they tried their best to tarnish his image.

As we left the courtroom that day, the judge and my attorney held the door open for me as I removed the cross from the federal courthouse. "Hey, Your Honor," I said in a playful manner, "need any lumber?"

"Ah, no, Reverend. I think you've found a very appropriate use for that lumber. I think what you're doing is, ah . . ." he scratched his chin searching for the proper word, "is very commendable."

"Did you hear that?" I asked my attorney later.

"What?"

"The judge commended me," I stated.

"Well, why am I not surprised?" he laughed, and we rejoiced, sensing victory was soon to be ours. Although a victory would be rightfully ours, we determined God would get all the glory, which is precisely what happened when the jury declared the defendants guilty of unlawful arrest, unlawful and excessive force, unreasonable conditions of restraint, assault, and battery. We were awarded a generous financial settlement to cover my medical and legal expenses and then some.

Aside from acquiring an appreciation for the apostle Paul's trials and tribulations, being beat up for preaching the gospel was not a fun experience. Yet when I look back and see what God did despite the devil's attempt to silence this street preacher, I become more determined to fight the good fight of faith. I can be as stubborn as God wants me to be.

> Being beat up for preaching the gospel was not a fun experience.

Nabbed for Nothing

Sometimes, however, arrests have happened closer to home. It was Saturday, the fifth of December, 1998, when a few Manassas, Virginia, police officers decided to take a stand against Christians singing Christmas carols at a Christmas parade. They must have felt it was their duty to save and protect citizens from a few fully devoted evangelicals who had come to celebrate Jesus, the reason for the season, and who brought with them a reminder that after the manger came a cross.

Our oldest daughter, Rachel, used a small public address system carried by a friend to lead the crowd in the Yuletide choruses. Our daughter Deborah offered tracts to people waiting along the parade route. I carried the cross. It was quite a shock when police officers on bicycles asked us to stop singing. It seemed ludicrous, considering this was my hometown.

"You'll have to stop doing what you're doing," the officer informed me.

"Who, us?" I asked the officer.

"Yeah, you. You can't do this."

"Why not?"

"You're demonstrating without a permit. You need to get a permit."

"Oh, I see. But officer, I do have a permit to do this."

"Where is it? Can I see it?"

He asked so I told him. "It's in the Library of Congress. It's called the Constitution of the United States of America, and I believe what I'm doing is covered under freedom of speech."

"Ah, well, you still can't demonstrate without a permit."

"Well, I'm not protesting or demonstrating against anything," I explained.

"What do you think you're doing?"

"Proclaiming!"

Not one policeman looked thrilled at the thought of having to deal with this situation, which was attracting more attention than we could have hoped for on our own.

"Look, you've got to do what you've got to do, but today's not the day I'm going to stop exercising my freedom of speech or freedom of religion."

"But the law in Manassas says . . ."

"Listen, I mean no disrespect, sir, but I don't care what law Manassas came up with. Do you realize it's illegal for Manassas to have a law on the books that's unconstitutional? Manassas should not have laws that supersede the Constitution. And whether or not you were responsible for creating that law, now that you've enforced it, you've become a breaker of the law. I've broken no law, but you, on the other hand, are now a lawbreaker."

"I don't think . . ."

"Well, I have thought about this. If you go ahead and arrest me, I'm gonna show up in court to fight this. This isn't the first time I've done this. I've been doing this for twenty years. I've never been convicted, never lost a case, and every time it happened that the police arrested me, the arresting officer has always gotten in trouble. In this case, that would be you! I'm talking about you."

"Listen, I've written this ticket up many times. They come to court, they pay their fine, and they don't come back. I've never lost one of these," he said confidently.

"Well, this is interesting. Apparently, there's coming a day one of us is going to have a first-time experience. If it's me, I gotta pay a fine. If it's you, who knows what price you'll pay. I just hope it doesn't cost you your job." With that, I signed the warrant and was legally charged with demonstrating without a permit.

Unbelievers Rally behind the Street Preacher

I turned to address the crowd. "Is there anybody here willing to testify in a court of law about what just happened here?" Hands shot up everywhere. The police officers looked at each other.

"Hey, can I get a picture of the preacher getting arrested?" someone shouted from the growing crowd.

"Sure," I said, "I think that would be just great!"

> "Hey, can I get a picture of the preacher getting arrested?"

While I collected names, addresses, and phone numbers, a guy came up to me and said, "Hell, I think you're great! Keep it up, man. Good work. Can I shake your hand? Man, I ain't believing this, a preacher arrested for singing Christmas carols at a Christmas parade!"

"Hey, preacher, look this way!"

"Hold on!" I shouted back. "Make sure you get the cross in the picture!"

"Oh, yeah, right. Get that cross where I can see it. Now, hold it!"

The police officer was determined. "You know, you could go downtown, get yourself a permit, and you'd be okay."

"Not today. Not in time for the parade. And why should I? I don't need one. That's like getting a permit to drive down the street. I'm already allowed to drive down the street."

"You need a permit."

"Are you saying that to walk down the street and call out to people, 'Good morning, folks! Have a great day!' I need a permit?"

"No, that's legal," he said.

"Oh, but if I say in the same exact manner and tone, 'Good morning, folks! God loves you! Think about Jesus! Nobody loves ya like Jesus!' or 'Jesus is the reason for the season!' then I'm illegal?"

"Yes, sir, that's where the problem comes in."

"So, it's not that I'm calling out to the crowd, it's what I'm saying that's a problem for you. My choice of words is what's causing you to arrest me. Sounds like religious discrimination to me."

"You got to understand, what you're doing has the potential to be a nuisance."

"Well, sir." I knew what was going to come out next.

I couldn't resist. "Again, I mean no disrespect, but you got to understand something, your sins *are* a nuisance to God and that's why Jesus was born! Merry Christmas!"

The confrontation was going pretty well, I thought, until they questioned me about the ages of my daughters. "You know, Mr. Nissley, because you have these minors, these young children, engaged in this illegal activity, there's more we could add to the charges."

The notion that as a street preacher in America I was contributing to the delinquency of minors was depraved! The implication that I could be construed as an unfit parent made my blood boil. Americans need to know how far their country has strayed from its godly heritage. I had to pinch myself and ask, *This is America, right?* Thank God someone cared enough to contact the mayor of the city of Manassas. The letter came to the mayor's desk from a friend of mine from Chicago when he caught wind of my arrest.

Dear Mayor Gillum,
I understand congratulations are in order. On December 5, 1998, your police officers were finally able to arrest and bring to trial the infamous Dr. Denny Nissley. And what is most surprising to me was that you were able to get him for singing Christmas carols at a Christmas parade! Disturbing the peace, I'm guessing. Someone told me it was because he was missing a permit. Could this be cor-

rect? I've known Denny for roughly fifteen years, and I've heard him sing. Though his voice is not "angelic," I don't think it merits arrest; however, there are a number of incidents you might be interested in:

1. In October of 1998, Denny loaded up his trucks with food and clothing and brought these much-needed supplies to the flood-ravished victims in Cuero, Texas. I understand he fed not only the people of Cuero, but also the utility and Red Cross workers who were there to restore order to the devastated community. I'm not sure if he cooked the food or not, but in all likelihood he most probably overlooked obtaining a permit. Also, I'm pretty sure the work he did to help put lives back together was not cleared through the union and may have violated someone's right to work.

2. Every year since I've known Denny Nissley he has spent time and energy organizing Christian outreach ministries to reach the people who wouldn't ordinarily go to religious services. He does this at great personal expense as he goes all over our nation. I've seen perfectly good alcoholics and homeless people transformed and changed by Denny Nissley's message of hope and the tangible love he offers. Perhaps you could nab him on some sort of meddling charge.

3. When I found out you were onto this guy, I was relieved. Finally, someone in authority knows

Denny has been bold enough to share the trans-
forming power of his faith to people like his neigh-
bor, an owner of a handful of porno shops in the
Washington, DC, area. God forbid this kind of man
becomes a good-hearted Christian and closes those
wonderful places of business. I maintain Nissley
must be stopped before his actions have a direct impact on the city's tax revenues!

I have many other stories to share with you
about this street preacher, but I've probably already
given you sufficient information about the character
of this man and the nature of his agenda.

Mr. Mayor, my sarcastic comments are intended
to help clarify the foolishness of arresting someone
for singing Christmas carols at a Christmas parade.
Might we agree that Denny's only oversight was
bringing the wrong prop? Perhaps he should have
carried a manger instead of a ten-foot cross.

> Sincerely,
> Kreg Yingst

The charges stemming from my arrest, which received
national attention in both the secular and Christian
media, were dismissed. The American Center for Law
and Justice released a press statement on March 1,
1999, stating that although they could not speak for the
Manassas City Attorney who did not specify his reasons
for dismissing the case, they felt it was wise for the City
Attorney to reconsider his decision to prosecute people

guilty only of exercising their right to speak about their religious beliefs in a public forum. I'm confident Manassas City Code 2-11 will be removed from the books after the attorneys from Virginia Beach finish what I started.

And now when one of the children starts singing in public, someone in the family remembers to call out, "Hey, be quiet! You'll get Daddy arrested!" In or out, when it comes to jail, all I have to do is sing. Nevertheless, I maintain a close relationship with some of the best attorneys in America.

CHAPTER NINE

Not Just Personal Disasters

A few years back, one of Christ In Action's board members, Pastor Allen Byerly of Thomasville Assembly in North Carolina, mentioned to Denny that he should consider helping out during disasters. Christ In Action has equipment for cooking and feeding on-site. With their generators and stage and 8,300 square foot tent, they can literally move in and set up a full-scale cooking and feeding site just about anywhere. And the mobile stage allows Denny and others to offer effective spiritual ministry after everyone's had a hot meal.

Street ministry IS disaster relief. Denny ministers to people who live in a disaster created by their life choices every day. However, the real reason Christ In Action has reached out to this area of need is very basic. Others have the need and Christ In Action has the ability to meet the need.

In October 1998 I was sitting at my computer in my office reading on the Internet about the flooding in southern Texas. The devastation was terrible. Twenty-six percent of the homes were destroyed in the town of Cuero, Texas, with 7,300 residents. There had never been a flood in the two-hundred-fifty-year history of the town, and now many homes were beneath fifty feet of water for over a week. The Lord began moving on my heart to do something.

About that time Sandy walked into my office and looked at my computer screen. Then she looked me in the eye and said, "You're going to Texas to do disaster relief, aren't you?"

I replied, "Yes, as soon as possible."

Sandy reminded me that it was Wednesday, and on Sunday we were going to have our son, Amos, dedicated. I cleared my throat, knowing that the church only does dedications every few months, and my wife wanted to do it at this time. The church had all the families lined up and ready for Sunday. *If we don't do it now, when can we?* I thought. I immediately called the church and asked for the pastor, who was not in. But, on hearing about my dilemma, his secretary asked me to hold for a minute. The next thing I knew I was hearing a man on the line talking in a real muffled voice. It was Pastor Nestor; he was at the oral surgeon's office having some major work done on his mouth. His secretary patched me through to him on a conference call. I briefly explained about going to Texas and about the baby dedication.

> The next thing I knew I was hearing Pastor Nestor at the oral surgeon's office!

"Wait till you get back" he mumbled almost inaudibly, "and then we'll do one just for you." On the ninth child, he figured, we rated our own baby dedication. This made Sandy happy, and I was set to go. Besides the baby dedication my pastor also said that the church would give the first $1,000 toward the relief effort. I asked Pastor if he would remember the conversation, as I was not sure how medicated he was, and with a chuckle he assured me he would.

I called Joe Randisi, a Christ In Action board member, who was working near his home on the interior of our stage trailer. I told him that I was planning to leave for Cuero as soon as possible. The stage wasn't ready yet, but he agreed to finish up as fast as he could. Five hours after seeing Cuero on my computer screen, I was leaving to meet Joe.

"Neither we nor Christ In Action has any money, you know," Sandy reminded me.

Concerned, I patted my pocket. "I have a credit card, and I can risk something for those who have lost everything." I put out a call for funds on our e-mail list and headed into the unknown territory of relief ministry.

As soon as I got on the road to meet Joe and the big truck, I started calling friends in Houston, asking for workers and food. I had helped Hugh Young launch His Shepherd's Staff, a street ministry working with the homeless of Houston. I also called Curt Williams, founder of Youth Reach Houston, a home for juvenile delinquent boys. They would work on resources while I drove.

I soon met up with Joe, and we took off for Texas. Joe drove our mobile commercial kitchen, and I drove the tractor trailer with the stage. In Georgia a truck driver on a CB radio asked what we were all about. I told him about our outreaches to the inner cities.

"But right now we're on our way to Cuero, Texas, to do disaster relief."

His response took Joe and me by surprise.

"Pull over at the next weigh station so I can give you some money," he told us.

I could not believe what I was hearing! I felt it was truly a sign from the Lord that He was going to meet all of our needs for this outreach. When we pulled up to the weigh station, the man handed me $75. Joe and I drove across the Georgia-Florida line rejoicing in what the Lord had done to provide for the trip. The entire trip ended up costing $7,500. That truck driver had provided our first one percent in cash. This was just the beginning of countless wonders the Lord would do on this outreach.

As we neared Houston, I contacted my friends again. Curt and Hugh had lined up thousands and thousands of pounds of food, bread, and cleaning supplies. Hugh found three workers at the local rescue mission. Two of them had just been saved the week before—one from a life of alcoholism, the other from a life of sexual and drug addictions. The third worker was not a Christian and was actively involved in the homosexual lifestyle. Curt sent me two boys and one staff member from the juvenile home.

"Can we win a city to Jesus with these guys?" I wondered out loud to Joe. It seemed impossible, but we knew God could do it.

We entered Cuero and set up in the middle of town to begin feeding people who had no more homes. As we were faithful to do all we could, the city officials asked us to be part of the official relief effort. We had to meet in the county courthouse every morning and evening to be briefed by the Emergency Operations Center and to report on our progress. We would also learn of other feeding sites that needed help. At the first meeting I was introduced and given a chance to speak. I commended the town council for their work and then shared with them that I wanted to bring Hope to Cuero, the Hope that is in Jesus. Everyone in the room began to applaud. I was nicknamed "the pastor of the disaster."

> Tracy turned out to be a dynamite on-site coordinator and a great barbecue chef.

The staff member from Youth Reach Houston, Tracy, turned out to be a dynamite on-site coordinator and a great barbecue chef. When a local physician offered six goats for a barbecue,

Tracy rounded up a smoker. Everyone around came for a feast!

Part of our job was to feed other relief workers. What a surprise when the warden of the local prison approached me to feed his inmates who were doing debris removal under tight security.

"I'd be delighted!" I replied.

When the first bus load of inmates arrived, I asked permission to address them. Onboard the bus, I welcomed them and explained the procedures for getting their meals. They would have to eat on the bus for security reasons. Then I gave them a brief version of my testimony, the story of my deliverance from drugs and alcohol.

I told them, "If it weren't for Jesus, I'd be imprisoned on this bus with you." After telling them how to be set free from sin and saved, I told them to file off the bus as I passed out copies of my testimony, "The Funnel." When the prison guard approached, I thought I was going to be reprimanded for preaching, but instead he asked to help pass out the tracts.

The Lord did many things through that first foray into disaster relief, but the best thing was that He confirmed in my heart that he wanted us to do His work in this way. We are not primarily a disaster relief ministry just as we are not primarily a children's ministry. But if we are available when disaster strikes, then we want to be there as Christ . . . in action.

By the time our work in Cuero was over, God had provided people to make donations to cover every penny of our work. His faithfulness never ceases to amaze me.

Oklahoma Tornadoes

God's faithfulness was again evident in Oklahoma after the tornadoes of the spring of 1999. The huge storm, with sustained winds of 318 miles per hour and gusts up to 400 miles per hour, had stayed on the ground for eighty miles. More than five thousand homes were completely destroyed and more than seven thousand more were damaged. Some forty-three people died.

The timing of the tornadoes was not good for our family. A number of people told me that I should not go to Oklahoma because we were in the middle of building a new home and Sandy was due to give birth to our tenth child. And, as usual, we had no money to make the trip. All this was true. Sandy was due to have a baby (Naomi Victoria was born June 20, 1999), and we sure didn't have the finances to make the trip. But what is faith? Going by what you see or by the leading of the Lord? Once again we followed God. The baby was born, the home still got built, and God provided an abundance of finances to cover the entire two and a half weeks of ministry.

> We were building a new home, and Sandy was due to give birth to our tenth child.

I called my former roommate from Christ for the Nations, Charlie, who works with the Assemblies of God church in Oklahoma City, and told him of my desire to help with the relief effort. He set us up with a man who owned a store and another man who owned a bar. The empty lot between their establishments was near one of the most devastated areas (Moore). Charles and his family joined our family in clearing the lot of debris. They had seven children and we had nine at the time, so it didn't take long to finish the task. Half of the empty lot was owned by the store owner and half by the bar owner. Someone asked why I would set up on the property of a bar to do the work of the Lord. My reply was that reaching that bar was part of why God sent us to Moore, Oklahoma. We were able to love on the managers and workers as well as all the patrons in the bar. We made many friends from that bar and made even more of an impact on the workers. Jesus will go to great lengths to reach lost souls. I'm proof.

During the Oklahoma relief effort, we had teams from Alabama, Virginia, West Virginia, Iowa, and Texas come to help. Sandy planned all the meals, and Rachel, our oldest, did the cooking. More than 2,000 meals were served. Bethany, Melody, Deborah, Leah, Elizabeth, and Grace helped with serving meals and cleaning up. Priscilla, who was only three, and Amos, one, helped by picking up trash and being cute.

Hurricane Flooding

Our next relief effort came in late 1999 when Hurricane Floyd unleashed his fury on the Carolina coast. I called board member Allen Byerly and asked if he would be able to put us in contact with a needy area. He called the North Carolina Assemblies of God District office and told them of the equipment and ministry of Christ In Action. They immediately went to work on a location and began recruiting helpers to assist us. This effort was Christ In Action sponsored by the North Carolina Assemblies of God. It was by far our most effective relief effort. Along with the teams that came from other states to assist us, we had hundreds of folk from the North Carolina churches.

We were able to set up in Tarboro, the hardest hit area in the state. This was the worst natural disaster in the history of North Carolina. Princeville, just on the other side of the Tar River from Tarboro, had been completely underwater—every one of their thirty businesses along with every home in town. Some of the officials from the district office were able to get us into Tarboro the very day they opened the town, and we set up in the parking lot of the old Tarboro Hospital. This hospital had sat empty for the last ten years and had been bought by two brothers from the town. They gave us permission to camp in their parking lot. The city was without uncontaminated water, and every restaurant was closed because they could not function without water. We began cooking and feeding in the name of the Lord and as of the second day we were cooking at least fifteen hundred meals a day. One morning Rachel cooked breakfast for over twelve hundred people before 9:30 A.M. Thank God we also had a cook from a nearby church. We provided nearly thirty thousand meals. It was a miracle that Rachel, seventeen, was able to come at all. For the last two and a half years she had suffered back problems. They had gotten worse during the Oklahoma relief effort and a mission trip to Mexico. The last doctor that saw her was amazed that she had actually walked into his office since the condition of her back was so bad. When the North Carolina relief trip arose, she was too debilitated to go along, so everyone stayed behind while Denny left to minister.

One night, disgusted with the devil's interference in her life, Rachel started doing spiritual warfare in prayer, bringing to God concerns about her friends and family members, but not her back! Then it occurred to her that she should include herself in her prayers. She did, and prayed for over two hours. Next morning when she awakened, she was without pain for the first time in years. Excited, she began picking up her sisters out of bed, something she'd been unable to do for months, to tell them about her healing. Then she called me and reached me in an Emergency Operations Committee meeting. She was so excited and pleased that I decided to go and pick up the whole family to join the relief effort that very day.

> One doctor who saw her was amazed that she had walked into his office.

Rachel put her back to the test, lifting up everything she could. She was like a person after a long fast who wants to eat everything in sight. She wanted to lift everything that wasn't nailed down. With Jack, a volunteer cook, she distributed meals to hundreds of people each day. I will never forget her hard work.

Another thing I will never forget in Tarboro occurred on the third day. Just before noon I was standing near the serving area when an elderly African American lady walked up to me and very timidly asked if we were serving food. I said, "Yes ma'am, we sure are, just step this way."

I began walking toward the serving table but I had to slow down and wait for her because she came to a stop just a few feet from the table. I gently bent over to be near her and asked if everything was all right. This dear woman shuffled her feet on the pavement and stuttered quietly. I was unable to hear what she was saying and bent even closer to her and asked her to repeat herself. I was jolted by her question. She asked, ever so humbly. "Do you all serve Black people?"

I could hardly believe what I heard. I thought, *This isn't 1952; it's 1999.* I wasted no time in responding. I reached out and took this dear lady by the arm and as I rubbed her skin I replied, "Ma'am, it isn't the color of your skin that matters. In whose image and likeness have you been made?"

This lady lifted her head up and looked me right in the eye and replied "God's."

I told her, "That makes you and me equal. Now let me get you something to eat."

She smiled and said, "Thank you." I'm convinced that people don't care how much you know until they know how much you care. In these outreaches of disaster relief we saw so many hopeless people find hope. Many came to know Jesus as Savior. It would take an entire book just to share all of the wonderful things the Lord has done in the disaster relief ministry. Terry Dohse, one of our staff members, and I began counting things we thought were miracles just in the first couple of days in Tarboro, and when we got to fifteen we stopped counting and just started rejoicing in what God had done. That is the way it is with God. He's too wonderful to comprehend. That's certainly what our children found out.

Fifteen-year-old Bethany, like Rachel, was a big help in North Carolina. She was also assigned to aid in the cooking, and she provided assistance from 5:00 A.M. to 10:30 P.M. daily, catching up on sleep during afternoon lulls.

Bethany was appalled by the devastation. On a tour of Princeville, she saw a house that was sitting askew on the road like Dorothy's house in *The Wizard of Oz*. The National Guardsman who was conducting the tour of the area told her that it had been across the whole road and

> On a tour of Princeville, Bethany saw a house askew on the road like Dorothy's house in *The Wizard of Oz*.

was bulldozed to the side so emergency vehicles could get by. Bethany wondered what had happened to the owners and if they were still alive.

Four days later she got her answer. While serving ribs she helped one woman carry her dinner back to her car. On the way they struck up a conversation, and Bethany learned that this was the owner of the house on the road. She was amazed to find out how grateful this woman was that her family had been spared injury, even though they lost everything else. When Bethany said, "God bless you," the woman responded, "He already has. God is good *all* the time."

Melody, thirteen, did a little of everything while in Tarboro. She cleaned abandoned hospital rooms so the volunteers could sleep there, washed dishes, and prepared and served food. "As hard and tiring as it was, I would do it all over again as long as it would bring hope and salvation to even one person," she declared afterward. Also amazed by what she saw on the tour of Princeville, she met one man who had barely made it out alive.

> "Thirty minutes later the water was eight feet deep."

"I woke up during the night, and the water was up to my ankles," he said. "I thought it might be time to leave. Thirty minutes later the water was eight feet deep!"

Eleven-year-old Deborah remembers that the Tar River had crested forty-three feet above flood stage.

When the National Guard took them through Princeville, she saw complete chaos created by water. "There
were chairs on top of houses, under houses, sitting on
fences. But a church sign with
removable letters was not missing a single one!" The guide
opened the door of a mobile
home that looked barely damaged on the outside. But inside
everything was trashed. In the graveyard, the crypts
were open and there was nothing inside. The caskets
had all floated away. There were so many needs to be
met, it could easily have become overwhelming. But
God took care of us.

> In the graveyard,
> the crypts were
> open but there was
> nothing inside.

We were so thankful for the Assemblies of God, their
help providing workers, and the tremendous assistance
they gave in administration and coordination of food
and volunteers. They also underwrote a great deal of
the finances. We had teams from many different de-
nominations rally around to help. Pentecostal and fun-
damental churches alike laid down their denominational differences at the foot of the cross and became
Christ . . . In Action.

CHRIST IN ACTION

Perhaps this book has given you a passion for taking the love of Jesus to where it is most desperately needed and hardest to find. Perhaps you want to know more about sharing the gospel on the streets of America. Or maybe you'd like to contribute to CIA's programs or join in one of their outreaches. Whatever your interest, feel free to contact us:

Christ In Action
P.O. Box 4200
Manassas, VA 20108

Website: www.christinaction.com